Early Steps
Learning From A Reader

TABLE OF CONTENTS

Chapter 1
The Beginnings

We worry about the three or four children in first grade who struggle with reading. As teachers, we know too well that having a poor start in grade one is just the beginning. Their problems only intensify as they progress through school.

Longitudinal studies tell us that low first grade readers will likely be the lowest readers in grade four (Clay, 1985). Even more troublesome is the research documenting that the gap between low and high readers broadens as children progress through the grades. Most low readers never catch up with their peers in reading and writing tasks. They are the ones who leave high school early. Most never become a productive part of society. What can we do to soften their struggle?

Let's begin to help these children before they ever know they are in trouble. Why not intervene early before they have a sense of failure and while the gap is still relatively narrow between those who are succeeding and those having difficulty? Many schools have responded to this challenge by implementing one-to-one tutoring programs for children classified at highest risk for reading problems.

In this book, I describe Early Steps, an early intervention program designed for accelerating the reading performance of at-risk first graders. The program has shown promising results. Not only do struggling first graders make strong gains in reading, but these effects are maintained through the grades (Santa & Høien, 1999). In a longitudinal evaluation of Early Steps we found that children participating in the program made significantly more growth in reading than did children in our regular Title One program. Moreover, these effects were most dramatic with the most at-risk readers. First graders participating in Early Steps, who scored the lowest on pre-tests measuring alphabet knowledge, concept-of-word, phonemic awareness and word recognition, made more progress than control children who were similarly at risk. Even more impressive was the finding that the experimental children were still progressing well in reading as third graders, two years after they had completed the program.

Early Steps History

Darrell Morris, a professor from Appalachian State University, began developing Early Steps while working with children with reading difficulties in an after school tutoring program. He and several colleagues initiated the Howard Street Tutoring program in a dilapidated store front in North Chicago. Children, mostly second graders from poor neighborhoods, walked to Howard Street and met after school for tutorial sessions with trained adult volunteers. For ten years Darrell trained and supervised the volunteers. You can find a complete description of the program in his well crafted and detailed tutoring manual, *Case Studies in Teaching Beginning Readers: The Howard Street Tutoring Manual.* (You will find ordering information in the bibliography.)

From this daily work with children and tutors, he began conceptualizing Early Steps, a program for assisting first graders with reading before they had an opportunity to fail. Early Steps represents a compilation of teaching practices from the Howard Street program and from the work of Edmund Henderson and Marie Clay. Since moving to Appalachian State University in Boone, North Carolina, Darrell has spread the program to a few school districts in the Northeast.

Several years ago Darrell agreed to assist us with implementing Early Steps in our local school district in Kalispell, Montana. I organized a graduate class through the University of Montana which he and I taught together. All teachers implementing the program took the class. For the first year Darrell worked with Title One tutors, first grade teachers, and principals from two schools. He felt strongly that for a program to take hold many teachers must be involved, particularly all first grade and title teachers within a school. He made five three day visits to our district. During these visits he observed and provided feedback on tutoring lessons and assisted me in leading the graduate class. He also trained me to become the on-site teacher trainer.

Since that time, all Title One teachers and most kindergarten, first and second grade teachers, elementary principals and resource teachers in our district have participated in the Early Steps training. Early Steps has changed the way we teach reading, not only for children at risk for learning how to read, but for all children. We owe Darrell a huge intellectual debt. He is a teacher in the finest sense!

Early Steps and Reading Recovery share many similarities. They are both one-to-one tutorial programs designed for at-risk first graders and are based on sound theory and practice such as reading and rereading of small books, writing, and strategy knowledge. However, a major difference between the programs is instruction in phonological processing. Early Steps embraces a far more systematic phonological component than Reading Recovery. With Reading Recovery, children are assumed to acquire phonological strategies through reading connected text and by writing. Phonological skills are taught as needs arise with the teacher assisting the child to work out words with sound boxes and other informal strategies.

With Early Steps children also apply their phonological knowledge in daily sentence writing as they work out words in their writing. In addition, a specific portion of the lesson is set aside strictly for word study where children systematically focus on increasingly complex levels of phonological understanding.

Children are identified for the Early Steps program through classroom observations and through an informal assessment administered individually during the first month of grade one (see chapter 2). Children scoring within the lowest 20% of children in their first grade classroom are placed in the program. These children receive 30 minutes of instruction per day from a trained teacher. They graduate from the program when they are reading at least average in their class.

The Early Steps lesson contains four parts: rereading familiar books, word study, sentence writing, and reading a new book. Each part of the lesson is nested in a powerful theoretical background. Before turning to some more details about the program, let's briefly overview each component and some of the theoretical support.

Lesson Components and Theoretical Support

1. **Rereading Familiar Books**. We begin the lesson with three small books the child has already read. The third book in the sequence is the new book introduced the previous day.

Theoretical support. Allowing children to reread builds fluency and provides the child with a heightened sense of confidence and motivation. Building fluency through rereading rests on a long line of research and on common sense. Considerable research supports the idea that a child's reading performance improves as a function of the amount of time reading (Anderson, Wilson, & Fielding, 1988). Just as athletes develop skill at their sports through practice, so do readers. Through rereading, children gain speed, smoothness, and automaticity (Dowhower, 1994).

The importance of rereading not only emerges from research stressing the time factor or the amount children read, but from research supporting the theory of automaticity. The theory of automatic information processing in reading defines the fluent reader as one who decodes text automatically, with little attention to figuring out individual words. When strugglers allot too much time to individual words, they have little attention left for comprehension. Their reading becomes off-balance, and as a result, comprehension suffers. Rereading leads to fluency and balance of attention so that strugglers begin to *feel* what it is really like to read proficiently.

2. **Word Study**. In the next five or six minutes of the lesson the teacher leads the child through a series of letter and/or word sorts depending upon the child's alphabetic and phonemic knowledge. For many children the first weeks of lessons involve learning how to name and write the letters. Once children have demonstrated knowledge of the alphabet, they next practice discriminating initial consonant sounds by sorting picture cards that represent different beginning letters.

After discriminating the sounds with pictures, the reader learns the initial letters corresponding to the picture names. Next, they progress to word sorting where they simultaneously examine visual and auditory patterns. They start with word families (rhyming patterns --*cat, fat, bat*) and progress through short and then long vowel patterns. As the child advances through the word sorts, the teacher reinforces the child's knowledge with spelling activities and games.

Theoretical support. While the progression of lessons will become obvious in the chapters that follow, it is important to understand that the phonological component of Early Steps has a strong theoretical base. First, phonological knowledge is critical to beginning reading. Marilyn Adams in her book, *Beginning to Read: Thinking and Learning about Print* (1990) brought together a vast amount of research about how children learn to read. Her central conclusion was that the "most critical factor behind fluent word reading is the ability to recognize letters, spelling patterns, and whole words effortlessly".

Second, the word sorting instruction of Early Steps teaches the child how to use consistent patterns in our language for recognizing words. Pattern instruction has stronger research support as a more effective approach to teaching decoding than does instruction in single-letter sounding. Teaching children single letter sounds followed by blending is devoid of meaning, abstract, and difficult for children to learn because it is isolated from real reading and writing. Moreover, single-letter sounding is inconsistent with how phonics actually works. Readers don't figure out words by sounding out each letter. Instead, they use word parts. Linguists also tell us that individual letter-sound correspondences are highly unreliable. Individual letters, especially vowels, make different sounds depending on the syllables in which they are embedded.

Critical to the phonics instruction in Early Steps is research indicating that vowel sounds while inconsistent as single units are quite consistent within larger units (Adams, 1990). Linguists have systematically analyzed the consistencies in our language and have provided specific information about what to teach. They describe the basic phonological units as onsets and rimes contained in syllables. The onset is the consonant or consonant cluster that precedes the vowel; the rime includes any vowel and consonants that follow. So in the words *cat* and *stick*, the onsets are /c/ and /st/ and the rimes are *at* and *ick*. It turns out that the vowels embedded in rime patterns are consistent and reliable, while single vowel sounds and rules are not.

Once students know some of these basic rime patterns, they can apply what they know to new situations. Good readers seem to discover this phenomenon. When examining the word recognition strategies of achieving readers, it is clear that they use letter clusters and units higher than single letters to decode words (Goswami, 1986).

Pat Cunningham (1995) described this higher unit strategy as decoding by analogy. When decoding unknown words, we attend to familiar patterns in words and decode them using the patterns as decoding chunks. For example, if students know the *at* pattern in the words *cat, hat,* and *fat,* they can learn to apply this knowledge to figuring out unknown words such as *chat.* Word identification is a combination of both word pattern knowledge and strategies for applying this knowledge. Both of these features are inherent within the word study program of Early Steps.

3. **Sentence writing**. The next step in the lesson is sentence writing. The child writes a sentence from his own experience. The teacher encourages him to write down the letter sounds he hears. The teacher assists by using sound boxes and by calling attention to specific letter sounds and words. After writing, the child rereads the sentence. Then, the tutor writes it on a sentence strip, cuts the sentence apart, and asks the child to put it back together.

Theoretical support. Writing and reading represent reciprocal processes and when used together advance the child's literacy development. Practitioners have long known that children have more success reading what they have written and learning sight words based on their own experiences (Stauffer,

1969). Moreover, writing is particularly important in a beginning reading program where the child applies segmentation of speech sounds and invented spelling to enhance phonemic awareness.

Encouraging children to write using the letters they hear is a powerful way to teach phonemic awareness (Calfee, 1991). Clarke (1988) compared the effectiveness of invented spelling versus an emphasis on correct spelling in first grade classrooms. The children using invented spelling were superior to others on measures of decoding at the end of the year. However, the effect was most striking with children initially identified as most at risk for learning to read.

4. **Introduction of a new book**. The lesson concludes with the introduction of a new book which the child is expected to read without much help the next day. The book is often at a slightly more advanced level than the books the child has previously read.

Theoretical support. In Early Steps, the children advance through a series of progressively more challenging books as they become more and more proficient with reading. We all know how important it is for children to have an opportunity to read books on their instructional level where they can profit from instruction (Morris, Shaw & Perney, 1990). Children learn most effectively in situations where they are challenged but not overwhelmed (Gambrell, Wilson & Gantt, 1981). Pacing children through increasingly challenging selections and time in reading practice, are key features of the program.

Previewing What's Ahead

With this overview of components and theory, let's now preview what lies ahead in the remaining chapters of this book. The next chapter features a description of the assessment administered to children during the first month of grade one. At this time, you will also meet Nick, a first grader featured for the remainder of this book. You will see his test results and how these results informed my instruction. Next, you follow Nick's progress through grade one and participate in the decisions that I made as his tutor. In each of the next three chapters, you observe Nick as he moves from being a non-reader to becoming quite proficient and in the process, learn about Early Steps through the perspective of one small, remarkable boy.

In the final chapter, I collaborate with Roxanne Gallup, a first grade teacher, in describing ways to implement Early Steps strategies into the regular classroom. She talks about why her teaching will never be the same.

There is also a video available with this book. Over a one year period I invited Randy Yearout from a local production company to video tape our lessons. Randy came to Nick's school about every six weeks during our regular tutoring time. The video contains five lessons beginning in October and concluding in June. After each lesson, I spend about ten minutes on the video reflecting about Nick's performance and discussing different aspects of our lesson. Ordering information for the video is included in the bibliography and on the inside of the back cover.

Chapter 2
The Early Reading Screening Instrument

We identify children for participation in Early Steps through an informal assessment administered to first graders during the first month of school. Children enter first grade with a variety of literacy backgrounds. Some are reading; others don't know the alphabet. Before beginning to teach, we must learn about each child's literacy knowledge.

The Early Reading Screening Instrument (ERSI), developed by Darrell Morris, is an invaluable tool for gathering information about beginning literacy skills (Morris, 1992). It is not only easy to administer, but it provides a clear portrait of a child's literacy knowledge and information critical to early reading success.

Several researchers have collected evidence about the measure's statistical validity. First, the test predicts later success in reading. Research studies indicate that the *ERSI* predicts end of first grade reading performance. Children scoring low on this measure will likely experience difficulty learning to read in a regular first grade classroom. Second, the *ERSI* has adequate content validity. Lombardino, DeFillipo, Saritsky and Montgomery (1992) found that the *ERSI* given to children near the end of kindergarten correlated .73 with the Woodcock-Johnson comprehension subtest administered to the same children at the end of grade one. Similar results occurred with rural North Carolina students. Scores from the *ERSI* given at the beginning of first grade correlated .70 with a passage reading test administered at the end of grade one. (Perney, Morris & Carter, 1997)

The *ERSI* takes about twenty minutes to administer and evaluates areas which researchers have found critical to early success with reading such as letter knowledge, concept-of-word, phonemic awareness, and word knowledge. More specifically, it provides answers to the following questions:

• What does this child know about the alphabet? Can the child recognize and produce upper and lower case letters?

• What about concept-of-word? Does the child know that individual words make up written language?

• What is the child's phonemic knowledge? Where is the child developmentally with spelling?

• Can the child read any words?

The ideal situation is to administer the *ERSI* to all first graders. First grade teachers usually request help so they can complete the assessment over several days. Tutors, classroom aids, and parent helpers can easily be trained to give the assessment.

If first grade teachers find if difficult to give the complete assessment to all their children, they must, at a minimum, administer it to children in the lower half of their classes. These children make up the pool of candidates for admission into Early Steps.

Determining the children in the lower half of class requires some informal evaluations during the first weeks of school. One way to do this is to administer the Alphabet Knowledge Subest from the *ERSI* to every child and use this as screening measure for selecting children who then take the complete battery. Children, who easily and fluently name and write the letters of the alphabet, are unlikely candidates for Early Steps. Alphabet knowledge tends to be quite predictive of later success in reading. Children, who come to school with letter knowledge, usually have other skills in place necessary for early reading success. Therefore, dividing children into those who have or do not have letter knowledge is a good place to begin.

Test Administration

Let's now turn to a step-by-step description of the *ERSI*. You will find a copy of the test in *Appendix A*. Also located in *Appendix A* is the student record form and abbreviated teacher directions. Refer to these items as you continue reading about how to administer and score the test. The teacher directions will be particularly helpful.

The assessment contains four tasks: *Alphabet Knowledge, Concept-of-Word, Phoneme Awareness*, and *Word Recognition*.

1. Alphabet Knowledge

The first section (1.1) evaluates letter knowledge. Children must be able to name and produce letters before learning to read and write. Children, who enter first grade with this knowledge, have an advantage compared to those unable to name and produce letters. Many letter names also carry the sounds represented by the letters (*d* makes the /*d*/ sound). Knowing letter names assists children in their early attempts with phonetic spelling necessary for beginning writing.

Administration. The *Alphabet Subtest* contains a random list of upper and lower case letters. Ask the child to name the letters as you point to them.

Scoring. On the student record form, section 1.1, note specific letter identification errors and no-attempts for both upper and lower case letters. (For more information on how to score, see section 1.1 on the abbreviated teacher directions.) Notice that reversals are counted as errors, but self-corrections are not. Also notice how letter identification errors are marked on the student record form. For example, if the child calls a *b* an *h*, write an *h* above the *b*. Also note whether the child does the task relatively quickly or more laboriously. The quicker and more accurate the response, the better.

Administration. For the *Production* assessment, ask the child to write the letters of the alphabet on a blank sheet of paper. Dictate the letter names in random order. The child can use either upper or lower case forms. Make a note on section 1.1 of the student record sheet of the letters he cannot produce.

Scoring. The scoring is identical to that described earlier for the alphabet recognition, except that left-right reversals are now counted as correct (*b-d*) but the up-down reversals (*p-d*) are still considered errors. Given that left-right reversals commonly occur with most beginning readers and normally take care of themselves over the next several months, they aren't counted as errors. However, the same is not true of up-down reversals (*u,n*). If not cleared up, they can become more problematic. Mark self-corrections as correct.

The child receives three subscores:

Recognition upper case (0-26)
Recognition lower case (0-26)
Production (0-26)

Interpretation. These subtests provide valuable information particularly when looking beyond the total score to the types of errors the child makes. For example, a child who makes only reversal errors on the recognition measure, is further along in alphabetic knowledge than a child who can't recognize an *M* or a *T*. Most children also find the capital letters easier to recognize and produce than lower case letters. These performance differences are quite understandable because the capital letters have more discriminative features than do the lower case forms. Therefore, a child having difficulty with both capital and lower case letters is further behind in alphabet knowledge than a child who knows most of the capital letters, but still has some problems with lower case letters. Finally, letter production is a more advanced task than recognition. If a child can recognize and produce most of the letters, he is well on his way to mastery. Take into account this qualitative information when examining a child's performance and use it to inform your own teaching.

Reflections about Nick. It is now time to meet Nick, the child featured throughout this book. Marilyn, Nick's teacher, immediately recognized him as a potential candidate for Early Steps. He had a way of standing out the very first day of school. Sitting and focusing on anything for more than a moment was not something Nick could do easily. He had trouble writing his name. Marilyn wondered if his observed problems with letter recognition might be because he couldn't sit still long enough to write, or if he really had difficulty. She wanted to know more about him. Was he simply lively or did he lack sufficient knowledge to learn how to read? Marilyn placed Nick first on her list for further evaluation.

Nick showed uncertainty with alphabet knowledge. His performance followed a predictable pattern. He had an easier time with the capital letters than with lower case and did better with letter recognition than with production. He also demonstrated a lack of fluency by taking longer than many children in naming and writing the letters. His hesitation

```
┌─────────────────────────────────────────────────────────────────┐
│ ┌───────────────────────────────────────────────────────────┐   │
│ │                    1.1   ALPHABET                           │   │
│ │                    X                    A        W          │   │
│ │ RECOGNITION:  A F K P W Z   B H O J U   C (Y) L Q M         │   │
│ │                        L                          ┌─────────┤   │
│ │              (D) N S X I   E G R (V)(T)           │# CORRECT 18/26│
│ │                                                   │   (a)   │   │
│ │                h b    x                  a        ├─────────┤   │
│ │              (E) f k p w z   b h o j u   c (y) l (q) m       │   │
│ │                        L              j e        ┌─────────┤   │
│ │              d n s x i   e g r (v) t              │# CORRECT 13/26│
│ │                                                   │   (b)   │   │
│ │ ─────────────────────────────────────────────────┴─────────┤   │
│ │                c t          D              i                │   │
│ │ PRODUCTION:  A F (k)(p) W Z  B H O (J) U  (c)(Y) L (q)(m)   │   │
│ │                                                   ┌─────────┤   │
│ │              D N S X I   (b)(g) R (V) T          │# CORRECT 11/26│
│ │                             V                     │   (c)   │   │
│ └───────────────────────────────────────────────────┴─────────┘   │
└─────────────────────────────────────────────────────────────────┘
```

coupled with his letter confusions and inability to name a significant number of letters provided critical teaching information. We needed to start with some alphabet work.

As mentioned earlier, many teachers use the *Alphabet Knowledge* subtest as a screening measure for identifying children for further evaluation. After administering the test to every child, teachers organize individual scores from highest to lowest and then divide their class into the upper and lower halves. Children in the lower half take the rest of the test.

If teachers have any concerns about an individual, they administer the complete battery to the child. Of course, the best plan is to administer the test to all first graders. Having a complete picture of everyone provides important information about individual needs and assists with planning instruction for small groups (see Chapter 6).

2. Concept-of-Word

Before children learn how to read, they don't need to know about single words in text. Most young children are unaware that the sentence, *I want to play with my friend*, has seven separate words. Yet, reading requires the matching of the spoken word to the written word. Until children can read a sentence and point to the individual words, they will have difficulty learning new sight words or attending to letter/sounds within single words (Clay, 1979, Morris, 1993). Therefore, it is important to find out if a child can point accurately to words as he reads.

Find the assessments for concept-of-word in sections 1.2 and 2.1 of the *ERSI*. The child sits next to you. Begin reading and pointing to each word. Next, ask the child to read and finger-point the same sentence. Some children will point to each word as they read; others will not. Notice the variety of possible responses as children read and finger-point:

- Some will move their hand quickly under the line of print without pointing to any word.
- Others may point to several words, but then lose track and skip to the end of the line.
- Some will stay with the text and point to each word as they repeat the sentence.

Staying with the text indicates an understanding of concept-of-word. The voice matches each word in the line of print. The other examples represent mismatches and a lack of understanding that the voice and the written words go together. After a few practice items, some children will begin to voice-match the words. Others won't.

The evaluation for concept-of-word actually includes two related tasks. The first task is like the one just described where the child rereads and finger-points the sentence just read. The second task involves naming a single word. After the child has finger-pointed and read the sentence, point to a single word in the sentence and ask him to read the word. Watch whether or not he can tell you the word.

At first, asking the child to go back and read a single word may seem more like an evaluation of word recognition or decoding ability. Yet, this isn't really what is happening. Most first graders don't come to us as readers. In order to do the task, they don't need to recognize the word. Instead, children can use sentence context and their memory of the text to pronounce a single word. Noting whether a child can finger-point words and then go back and read a specific word with contextual support lets us know if the child can match a printed word to the spoken word. The task ends up being a straightforward and accurate way to measure concept-of-word.

Administration. The assessment involves reading two small books: the *Katie* selection and *My Home* (by June Melser, published by the Wright Group in Bothell, Washington).

Directions: Book 1--*Katie*

- Take out the *Katie* selection. Sit next to the child. Before reading the story, look at the pictures and talk about what is happening on each page. Include in your conversation words contained in the story.

Then begin with modeling:

"This sentence (point to it) tells about the drawing. Watch while I read and point to each word. (Read and finger-point the sentence). Now, I want you to read along with me. (The child joins you in reading as you read and finger-point the sentence.) OK, this time you read the sentence and point to the words by yourself." (If necessary move her finger to the first word, *Katie* to get her started.)

After completing the first sentence, point to the target word in the sentence and ask, "Can you read this one?" Then move to the second word and ask, "What about this one?" Notice the target words are underlined on the student record sheet. Continue following the same procedure for the next three sentences. Read and finger-point. Then, ask her to do the same. After each sentence, point to the target word to see if she can read it.

Scoring. Notice on the student record form that the child gets two scores: one for reading and finger-pointing and another for reading the underlined word. Note whether or not she succeeds on both parts. Fill in the scoring sheet as she completes each sentence. Score finger-pointing attempts in an all-or-none manner. If the child finger-points the sentence correctly, she receives one point. If not, record a zero. She also receives one point for reading each underlined word. The word identification must be the exact word. For example, if she says *walk* for *walking*, record a zero but make a note of her attempt. It shows that she is getting close!

Testing Sequence. If you are following the suggested sequence for administering this battery, the next test is 1.3, *Word Recognition of Basal Words*. Yet, to make our discussion here a bit smoother, we will momentarily put off a description of test 1.3 and describe the other concept-of-word test. It's less confusing to discuss them together given they are eventually scored as one test.

As just mentioned for testing purposes, we don't administer the *Concept-of-Word* 1.2 and *Concept of Word* 2.1 in sequence. Instead, we break up these two subtests with test 1.3. In fact, after administering subtest 1.3, *Word Recognition of Basal Words*, it's best to end the testing session. (Notice how the test sequence is numbered--all of the number 1 tests are for the first session, the number 2 tests are for the second session.) Later during the day or within a few days, give the rest of the tests (2.1 *Concept-of-Word*, 2.2 *Phoneme Awareness* and 2.3 *Word Recognition*) to the child. At the beginning of the school year, giving the entire battery in one sitting is too exhausting for the child. Dividing the sessions gives a more accurate picture of what a child can do.

Directions: Book 2--*My Home*

Begin by sharing the book with the child. Look at the pictures and talk about what is happening on each page. Then, return to the first page and begin reading the book. You read and finger-point the first page. The child then does the same thing. Record on the answer sheet whether or not she actually points to each word (1 or 0). On reaching page 3 in *My Home,* tell the child to read the rest by herself. If the child cannot, continue to model and finger-point. Word identification checks occur on the first two sentences but not on the last three. See the underlined words on the student score sheet--*here* on page 2, and *is* on page 3.

Scoring: Combine the scores for the two selections. The two scores are the number of sentences read and finger-pointed correctly (0-8) and the number of target words identified (0-8). A perfect score is 16.

Interpretation: If a child can read and point to each word accurately and easily, she has internalized concept-of-word. On the other hand, if she cannot stick to the text, she doesn't really understand what a written word is. She might, for example, say the sentence quickly and run her finger beneath the line of print without really pointing to the words, or she might lose track and skip her finger to a word that she is not saying.

First graders begin school with varying abilities on being able to read the target words. Some show clear use of context by going back and rereading the line of print in order to identify the word. Others won't be able to do this. Gathering such information on individual children is critical because they must be able to match the spoken word to the printed word in order to learn how to read.

Reflections about Nick: As noted on the next page, Nick performed inconsistently with both tasks. However, by the second subtest (*My Home*) his concept-of-word seemed to be emerging. He read and finger-pointed every sentence correctly except for the last one and even succeeded in reading one of the test words. Because his performance improved, he will probably

```
┌─────────────────────────────────────────────────────────────────┐
│  ┌─────────────────────────────────────────────────────────────┐ │
│  │            1.2   CONCEPT OF WORD   ("Katie" Book)           │ │
│  │                                                             │ │
│  │                           Point      Words                  │ │
│  │              1        2                                     │ │
│  │  1. Katie is walking in the rain.    O  1 O 2 ✓            │ │
│  │              1        2                        ┌──────────┐ │ │
│  │  2. She sees a big dog.         ✓ 1 O 2 O      │Scores are combined with section │
│  │              2        1                        │2.1. When test is completed, │
│  │  3. The dog shakes water on Katie.  O 1 O 2 O  │count ✓'s for pointing & words.│
│  │                                                │Record in box in section 2.1.│
│  │                                                └──────────┘ │ │
│  └─────────────────────────────────────────────────────────────┘ │
│                                                                   │
│  ┌─────────────────────────────────────────────────────────────┐ │
│  │            2.1   CONCEPT OF WORD   (My Home)                │ │
│  │                                                             │ │
│  │   Page                        Point.  Word                  │ │
│  │   (2)  My home is here,         ✓    ✓                      │ │
│  │        said the bird.                                       │ │
│  │   (3)  My home is here,         ✓    O                      │ │
│  │        said the frog.                    ┌────────────────┐ │ │
│  │   (4)  My home is here,         ✓        │Note: Count ✓'s for pointing│
│  │        said the pig.                     │& words from sections 1.2 and│
│  │   (5)  My home is here,         ✓        │2.1 and record totals below.│
│  │        said the dog.                     │                │ │ │
│  │   (7)  My home is here,         O        │# CORRECT(point.) 5/8│
│  │        said the rabbit,                  │              (d)│ │
│  │        and in I go.                      │# CORRECT(word.) 2/8│
│  │                                          │              (e)│ │
│  │                                          └────────────────┘ │ │
│  └─────────────────────────────────────────────────────────────┘ │
└─────────────────────────────────────────────────────────────────┘
```

learn this skill fairly quickly. With a little practice he already did better. This improvement indicates that Nick is a bit shaky with the task, but close. With more print experience, he should be there within a few weeks. However until then, he will make limited progress in learning how to read.

3. Phonemic Awareness (Spelling)

In order to read, children must first segment words into phonemes. Research documents that differences in phonemic awareness predict differences in early reading achievement. For example, if a child is aware of the beginning, middle, and ending phonemes in the word, cat ($/k/$ $/a/$ $/t/$), he will more quickly learn to read than a child only aware of the beginning sound in a word.

Spelling is a straightforward evaluation of phonemic awareness. Morris and Perney (1984) showed that a spelling test given to first graders at the beginning of first grade was a stronger predictor of year-end reading achievement (r=.68) than a reading readiness assessment (r=.34)

The assessment for phonemic awareness is a twelve word spelling task. Children write the sounds they hear in the words. Scoring involves counting the number of phonemes children write for each word. Six of the words in the test contain three phonemes (*back, feet, mail, chin,* and *road*) while the others have four phonemes (*step, junk, picking, dress, peeked and lamp*).

Administration. Start by modeling two practice items (*mat* and *lip*) and then read the words on the list, but offer no help in spelling them. Your modeling should go something like this:

Take the pencil in your hand and say, "We are going to write the word *mat*. Say the word *mat*. What letter do you hear at the beginning? What letter should I write down first?" Offer praise for the correct response, *m*, as you write the letter down. If the child gives the wrong letter, say "The first letter is an *m*," and write it down. "What letter should we write down next? Say the word again. What letter do you hear at the end?"

SCORING GUIDE FOR SPELLING

EARLY READING SCREENING INSTRUMENT
SECTION 2.2 PHONEME AWARENESS

One point is awarded for each phoneme represented by an appropriate letter. Examiners will need to interpret spellings if no example below matches child's attempt. Phoneme's represented out of order are not awarded points. Note maximum points per word varies from 3 to 4.

	Points	1	2	3	4
1	back	B, BN	BC, BK, BA, BAE BIG, BOC	BAC, BAK, BAKE, BACK	
2	feet	F, FA	FT, FE, FIT	FET, FEAT, FETE, FEET	
3	step	S, C, SOT	ST, CP, SA, SE	STP, SAP, CAP, CAP, STIP	STAP, STEP
4	junk	J, G	JK, GC, JO, GU	JOK, GOK, GNK, JIJK	JONG, GUNK
5	picking	P, P0	PK, PC, PE, PN	PEC, PEK, P1K, PEN, PKN	PECN, PICEN, PEKN, PICKING
6	mail	M, MI	ML. MA, MAO, ME	MAL, MAOL, MALE, MEL, MAIL	
7	side	5, C, ST	SE, CD, SA, SED	SID, CID, SAD, SOD, SIDE	
8	chin	G, J, H	GN, IN, HN, GAN	GEN, HIN, CHEN, CHIN	
9	dress	D, J, G	JS, GS, DOS	JAS, DES, IRS, DRS, DESS, GAS	DRAS, JRES, DRES, DRESS
10	peeked	P	PT, PE, PK, KIT	PET, PCT, PEK, PIKT, PEET	PECT, PEKED, PEEKT, PEEKED
11	lamp	L	LP, LA, LOP, LM	LAP, LAPE, LAM, LMP	LAMPE, LAMP
12	road	R, W, RT	RD. RO	ROD, ROED, RODE, ROAD	

* printed with permission of Darrell Morris

Continue with the next sample word, *lip*. After demonstrating the two examples, give the pencil to the child and say:

"Now I am going to read some words. Try to write them. Write the sounds you hear." Then, read the words on the list, but offer no help in spelling them. You can, however, remind the child to say the words as he writes.

The Table on the left summarizes the scoring system. One point is awarded for each phoneme represented appropriately.

The following is an example of one child's (Bradley's) performance on the spelling assessment as well as the scores for each item. While scoring will be subjective, given that children always invent their own versions of words, stay as closely as you can to the scoring as outlined in the guide. Notice that reversals are counted as correct.

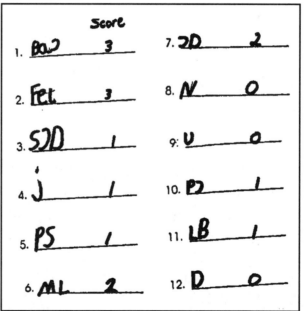

Interpretation. One way to interpret this test is according to the stages of spelling development. A child's early writing is filled with spelling errors that are very interesting. These errors are both smart and predictable. When understanding the logic of children's errors and the thinking strategies behind this developmental progression, we gain insights about ways to assist children toward mastery.

It is interesting to note that the same developmental error patterns occur irrespective of intelligence, economic class or language. The pace among high and low achievers differs, but every child follows a similar course. Moreover, the error patterns do not differ according to instruction.

The first stage is *Preliterate* where the child writes using a combination of scribbles, letters, and numbers. Stage 2 is *Semi-phonetic*. Children use letter names to represent one-syllable words with beginning and sometimes ending consonants. The names of many consonants are actually close to the letter sounds. Therefore, children represent them quite directly (*BK=back, FT=fat*). By stage 3 (*Phonetic*) they start using letters names to represent the long vowels fairly accurately and begin experimenting with short vowels (*BOT=boat, CAK=cake*). Short vowels are also represented by the letter name which most closely approximates the sound of the letter. When children reach stage 4 (*Transitional*), they represent the short vowels correctly as well as many of the long vowel patterns. The table below gives typical spelling attempts according to stages 2, 3 and 4 for the words on the *ERSI* (Morris, 1992).

Spelling	Semi-phonetic	Semi-phonetic	Phonetic	Transitional
back	B	BC	BAC	
feet	F	FT	FET	FETE
step	S	SP	STAP	STEPE
junk	J	GK	JOK	JUNCK
picking	P	PKN	PEKN	PICING
mail	M	ML	MAL	MALE
side	S	SD	SID	SIED
chin	C	HN	CHEN	
dress	D	JS	JRAS	DRES
peeked	R	PT	PEKT	PEAKED
lamp	L	LP	LAP	
road	R	RD	ROD	RODE

Developmental Stages in young children's spelling
(from Morris, 1992, p 48)

In examining the previous student example, Bradley fits within the *Semi-phonetic* stage of development. He was inconsistent in spelling beginning sounds and sporadic with ending sounds. Yet, he also has some real strengths. He has some knowledge of consonant sounds which means that he will probably progress quite quickly in learning all of them. Now, let's talk about Nick's performance.

Reflections about Nick. Nick had tremendous difficulty with the spelling task. In fact, he was unable to spell any of the words. He had no idea how to segment words into phonemes and represent any of the letters. Given his difficulty with the previous test on *Alphabet Knowledge,* his performance here is predictable. His performance has not reached the level of *Semi-phonetic.* We needed to start at the beginning with learning letters and the sounds of the initial consonants.

Children, who perform well on this subtest, are far more likely to become good readers than children like Nick. The spelling assessment turns out to be a sensitive measure for determining which children need early help with reading.

4. Word Recognition

Some children begin first grade knowing a few sight words. Early readers, who have a rudimentary knowledge of some words, certainly have an advantage compared to children who don't know any words. The assessment for word recognition contains two word sets. One is a list of common sight words (Basal Words, subtest 1.3) and the other contains a set of more decodable words (Decodable Word, subtest 2.3).

Administration. Point to the words, one at a time and ask the child to read them. If she is clearly frustrated, do the first three or four words and then stop. Reassure her. "You are only in grade one and I don't really expect that you will know any of these words, but let's give them a try. Can you read this word?" Record her attempts, particularly if she tries sounding-out the word. Remember, look beyond the total score. The child who says *came* for *come* is further along than a child who calls it *elephant.*

Follow the same procedure for the second list. These words follow a consonant-vowel-consonant pattern which gives children with some phonemic awareness an opportunity to read some of them. Again transcribe any of the child's attempts.

Scoring. Score each list separately. Ten points are possible for each. The child gets one point for each word pronounced correctly. It is also important to record attempts in pronouncing the words. Even though these attempts don't count into the score, they provide important diagnostic information. If the child comes up with a word that begins the same as the word on the list, he has more phonemic knowledge than one who simply makes wild guesses.

Reflections about Nick. I didn't even attempt this test with Nick. Given his difficulty with earlier parts of the test, I knew that giving him this word list would only frustrate him.

This subtest turns out to be quite useful for identifying children who don't need to be in an early intervention program. If children do quite well in the previous subtests, I definitely recommend giving this subtest. When children can identify four or five words on this test and succeed in making errors that phonemically match the target words, you can rest assured that they should progress well with regular classroom instruction.

Total Scores

Use the formula below to calculate the grand total. The formula converts the subtest scores so that each contributes up to ten points making a total of 40 points. Transfer the scores into the formula, calculate them and then add the four scores together for the grand total. Nick's grand total was 9.8. He performed the lowest in his class.

CALCULATING TOTALS	
ALPHABET $\left(\frac{a+b+c}{78}\right)$ x 10 = TOTAL	PHONEME AWARENESS $\left(\frac{f}{42}\right)$ x 10 = TOTAL
CONCEPT OF WORD $\left(\frac{d+e}{16}\right)$ x 10 = TOTAL	WORD RECOGNITION $\left(\frac{g+h}{20}\right)$ x 10 = TOTAL
Round to nearest tenth: .05's round up. Add four TOTALS to calculate GRAND TOTAL.	

SCORES										
ALPHABET			**CONCEPT OF WORD**		**PH. AWARE.**	**WORD REC.**				
Up	Low	Prod.	Point	Word	Count	Bas	Dec			GRAND TOTAL
26	26	26 TOTAL	8	8 TOTAL	42 TOTAL	10	10 TOTAL			
18	13	11 (5.4)	5	2 (4.4)	0 (0)	0	0 (0)			9.8
(a)	(b)	(c)	(d)	(e)	(f)	(g)	(h)			

$$\frac{18+13+11}{78} \times 10 = 5.4$$

$$\begin{array}{r} 5.4 \\ 4.4 \\ \hline 9.8 \end{array}$$

$$\frac{5+2}{16} \times 10 = 4.4$$

Once total scores are calculated, teachers find it helpful to rank order their children accordingly. The results provide a portrait of a class and baseline data for each child. The table on the adjacent shows the performance of children in Nick's class.

SCHOOL _____   TEACHER _____   DATE _____

NAME	ALPHABET				CONCEPT OF WORD			PHONEME AWARENESS		WORD RECOGNITION			GRAND TOTAL	Teach Rank
	Up. 26	Low 26	Prod. 26	TOTAL	Point 8	Word 8	TOTAL	Count 42	TOTAL	Bas 10	Dec 10	TOTAL		
Jordan	26	26	26	10	8	8	10	42	10	9	10	9.5	37.5	1
Amber	25	23	26	9.5	8	8	10	37	8.8	3	2	5.0	33.3	2
Jackson	26	25	26	9.9	8	8	10	25	7.3	2	3	2.5	30.7	3
Michael	26	25	26	9.9	8	8	10	31	7.4	1	3	2.0	29.3	4
Edward	26	24	24	9.5	8	7	9.4	35	8.3	1	3	2.0	29.2	5
Allison	26	24	26	9.7	7	6	8.1	31	7.4	1	1	1.0	26.2	6
Kayla	26	24	24	9.5	7	4	6.9	30	7.1	0	0	0	23.9	7
Sarah	25	24	24	9.4	6	5	6.8	25	6.0	1	1	1	23.3	8
Manda	24	24	24	9.2	7	3	6.3	21	5.0	1	1	1	21.5	9
Samuel	26	22	24	9.2	4	5	5.6	19	4.5	0	0	0	19.3	10
Derick	25	23	26	9.5	6	2	5	16	3.8	0	0	0	18.3	11
David	26	21	22	8.8	7	4	6.9	7	1.7	0	0	0	17.4	12
Bradley	26	24	24	9.5	6	1	4.4	14	3.3	0	0	0	17.2	13
Pete	25	22	24	9.1	2	2	2.5	21	5.0	0	1	.5	17.1	14
Mary	23	21	19	8.1	4	4	5.0	12	2.9	0	0	0	16	15
Trevor	23	20	20	8.1	4	4	5.0	8	1.9	0	0	0	15.0	16
Cortney	25	22	20	8.6	2	3	3.1	16	3.8	0	0	0	14.7	17
Bobby	22	19	20	7.8	3	3	3.8	5	1.2	1	1	1	13.8	18
Laura	24	20	21	8.3	1	1	1.3	15	3.6	0	0	0	13.2	19
Heather	20	21	22	8.1	2	2	2.5	11	2.6	0	0	0	10.6	20
Nick	18	13	11	5.4	5	2	4.4	0	0	0	0	0	9.8	21

Reflections about Nick. The *ERSI* clearly indicates that Nick is a candidate for Early Steps. Placing Nick in a regular classroom reading situation without any extra help would be disastrous. He simply does not have the skills to make good progress.

Planning for Instruction

Grouping decisions. In examining the class chart, roughly divide the class into thirds. The six children scoring above 25 points have excellent skills for becoming readers. They have alphabet knowledge, an understanding of concept-of-word, can represent letter sounds quite accurately in their writing and even have some word knowledge. These children are ready to begin formal reading instruction and should progress rapidly.

The children falling within the mid-range scoring from 23.9 to about 18.3 have some instructional needs with letter recognition and production, are not as adept with concept-of-word, and have fewer phonemes in their writing. Most had little if any word knowledge. These children will probably progress fairly well in grade one, but they must be closely monitored.

The children falling within the lower third of the class, particularly those scoring 16 or lower on the *ERSI*, will need immediate assistance learning their alphabet and their initial consonant sounds. The lowest four or five children would best be served in an early intervention program such as Early Steps.

Continual evaluation. Portions of the *ERSI* can also be administered several times during the school year as an objective measure of the child's individual growth. For example, after several weeks of instruction, pull children into a small group and give them the *Alphabet Production subtest*. In this way, you can find out exactly what letters you still need to teach.

Constantly re-evaluate children who were unsure of concept-of-word at the beginning of the year. Sit beside the child and find out if she can now reread and finger-point sentences.

The spelling assessment is an extremely useful tool for monitoring performance throughout the year. Many first grade teachers administer it at the beginning of the year and then several times throughout the year as a measure of a child's growth in spelling and phonemic awareness during first grade. The example below compares Bradley's spelling performance at the beginning to his performance at the end of grade one. What better way for a child to see his own remarkable growth. "Did I really begin the year spelling like that?" Date and keep the tests in the child's portfolio as documentation for the child and his parents.

Closing Comments

In conclusion, the *ERSI* provides rich information about first graders. Teachers immediately know the children who can begin formal reading instruction and those who aren't yet ready to learn how to read. Knowing about the literacy skills in a first grade class lets teachers know what they need to teach and the children in need of additional help during those first weeks and months of the school year.

Every child deserves to have a successful first grade experience. First graders have just begun the most important school year of their lives. Take time to administer the *Early Screening Reading Inventory*. If we catch children before they ever know they don't know, think what a difference we can make in their lives! Remember, we can't fix what we don't see.

Chapter 3
Fall

We begin tutoring first graders immediately after completing the assessments. We start with the children whose scores on the *ERSI* fall within the lowest 20% of the class. These children receive a half hour of tutoring per day. About 1/3 will exit the program midyear which leaves space for admission of other first graders making slow progress in reading, but who tested higher at the beginning of the year or entered grade one later in the year.

Preparing Materials

Before beginning the program in the fall, we collect and organize our lesson materials. We have a set of leveled books which can be shared among one or two teachers. The ideal situation is for every teacher to have one set of books, but given the expense of each set (approximately $1000) this is sometimes impossible. A bibliography of books and ordering information is in *Appendix B*. (Another excellent resource for leveled books is the bibliography found in *Guided Reading* by Irene Fountas and Gay Su Pinnell. The book levels are not the same as those designated by Reading Recovery. If you already have a series of leveled books available to you, feel free to use these rather than the books recommended in Appendix B.)

Leveled books

As noted in the bibliography, each level contains 10 to 15 books. The books begin at level one and progress to level 12. This list represents a collection of books from many different publishing companies. Darrell Morris and his colleagues have established the books into levels of sequential difficulty.

Children start by reading level one and two books. These easy books have pictures going along with the print, contain only one line of print per page, and follow a predictable pattern. Most are six or seven pages in length. The predictability of the text and the pictures assist children in reading the books. In fact, after one or two readings, most children have the books memorized. These first books invite children to read and assist them with acquiring concept-of-word and in learning some sight words.

Books on levels 4 and 5 continue to be fairly predictable but contain more print--from two to four lines on each page.

By the time children reach levels 7 and 8, the books have from five to six lines of print per page and are 10 or 12 pages in length. Because the text is less predictable, the child must rely more on word knowledge.

Little Brother, The Monsters' Party , and Who Will Be My Mother reprinted by permission of the Wright Group, Bothell, WA

Books on level 9 and higher are no longer predictable, contain more print on the page and have pictures that don't as precisely illustrate the text. At this level, the child must rely more on word knowledge, context, word patterns, and letter sounds.

Using a magic marker, we write the numbers of the book level on the back cover of each book and organize them into dishpans. We found that putting the numbers on the back was better than the front so that children became less aware of the level they were reading.

Sentence book

Nick and I began the year with four blank sentence books, which I made by stapling together about 15 sheets of paper into construction paper covers. Nick used one page each day for his sentence writing. We only used one side of each page, so that we had room on the back of the previous page for any extra work related to the sentence Nick was writing. This work might be figuring out words using sound boxes or practicing on letter formation.

Word and Letter Sort Cards.

I duplicated the letter, picture, and word masters included in Appendix C on heavy paper similar in weight to file folders. Then, I laminated them and cut them apart using a paper cutter. I organized the letter, picture cards, and word sort cards into a file box--a box used for computer disks tends to work well. I ordered the letter and picture cards alphabetically and the word sort cards according to the sequence of words sorts listed at the end of this chapter. For example, my short *a* families came first, followed by the short *i*, etc. Having all of the materials ready before beginning the tutoring meant less time spent planning and organizing during the school year.

Beginning Instruction

Nick turned out to be an ideal child to feature in this book. He started as the most at-risk child in his class with the lowest score on the screening instrument. In addition to his low performance, Marilyn, his first grade teacher, worried about his inability to attend. Nick struggled to sit in his chair and couldn't focus on either small group or large group lessons. Even though he had attended a strong program in kindergarten and received tremendous support at home from two highly literate, nurturing parents, he was not ready for the literacy demands of grade one.

I taught Nick for thirty minutes just after the morning recess. My choice of time was no accident. He needed recess to burn-off excess energy before our lesson. Thirty minutes of intense instruction is a long time for any first grader-- particularly for a child like Nick, who finds attending to practically everything related to school a challenge. Meeting at the same time and place each day was important not only for Nick, but for Marilyn. Consistency meant less disruption for her and her other first graders.

At the beginning of grade one Nick recognized 18 upper letters and could write eleven letters. He exhibited a beginning awareness of concept-of-word but couldn't represent any phonemes correctly on the spelling measure. A review of his assessment told me where to begin. We had lots of work to do.

On the very first day, we started a shortened version of the four-step lesson. We began by reading two level one books together. Before reading, we took a picture walk through each book and talked about what was happening on each page. Then, we went back to the beginning of the book. I read and finger-pointed the title with him and then echo read where I read a page followed by him reading and finger-pointing the same page. The books are so predictable that he ended up reading the last two or three pages of each book himself. After our reading, I explained that we would be reading these same books tomorrow.

Next, we did the word study portion of the lesson. I started by asking Nick to write his name--which he did perfectly. I then wrote it on a sentence strip, cut it apart, and we played a quick game of putting the letters back together. He also practiced saying the letters in his name in random order. Given that he had difficulty naming the letter *c* on the screening measure, he needed this work.

I explained that every day during our lesson he was going to write a sentence. For this first day, I told him that I would help him write. I asked, "What might be something you write about today?"

Nick said, *"I love my mom."*

I took the pencil and said, "How do you think I might write the word *I*?" He had no clue. "You write it like this". Next, we worked on *love*. "Let's say the word slowly. What sound do you hear at the beginning?" He guessed incorrectly, so I wrote down the *l*. As I wrote, we talked about the letter names and how to write them. I continued modeling the writing of the first letter, and said, " I wrote my sentence by thinking about the sounds of each letter. Tomorrow you get to write your own sentence."

Next, I introduced him to a third book and explained that we would be reading all three books again tomorrow. This first lesson lasted approximately 20 minutes which was about all Nick could take. We put our things away and talked about how we would be meeting each day at this same time.

Day Two

Rereading Familiar Books

We started the next day by rereading the three books introduced the previous day. I modeled again the first one or two pages of the book and then asked him to read the book, finger-pointing to each word as he read. When he had difficulty finger-pointing, I took his hand and showed him how to point to each word while reading. After holding his hand and echo reading the first several pages, he read and finger-pointed the rest of the book by himself. We also practiced naming some individual words. Directly after reading two or three pages, I pointed to a word and asked him to tell me what the word was. After one or two trials, he began to understand how he had to go back and finger-point the sentence until he came to the word.

Both of these tasks, finger-point reading and returning to the text to locate a specific word, helped Nick start to understand concept-of-word. Nick, however, didn't really begin understanding concept-of-word until he started reading harder level 3 and 4 books. It is difficult to see the need for concept-of-word when you only have two or three words per page. Children need more words on a page to understand the relationship between seeing and saying individual words. Therefore, by the end of our first week of lessons I had already moved Nick to level two books which still had high predictability, but contained several more words per page.

Letter Names

By this second day, we again reviewed the letters in his name. We worked on naming and writing them. As he wrote, he said each letter aloud. Then I dictated the same letters randomly and he wrote them again. We also mixed-up the letter cards and practiced matching upper and lower case letters.

Next, we played concentration. Nick placed all of the letter cards in his name face down. He drew a card and said the letter name. Then, he picked up another card, said the letter and decided if the letters matched. If the cards matched, he kept them. If not, he put them both back, face down on the table, and I took a turn. We continued until no cards remained on the table. If either of us forgot to name the letters as we turned over the cards, we lost our turn. The person with the most matching cards won.

This entire sequence focusing on letters took about six minutes. In fact, I made sure to limit the letter or word study portion of our lesson to not more than six to eight minutes. This is enough. I also reinforced letter knowledge during other parts of the lesson such as during book reading. For example, we would find all of the *c's* on a page.

Sentence Writing

"What do you want to write about today, Nick?" We talked about some ideas. Our conversation turned to skiing. "Now, let's see if you can put your ideas into one sentence."

With some help, Nick said, "I like to ski."

"TERRIFIC! Say your sentence again, and let's count the number of words". As Nick repeated the sentence, we counted the words on our fingers. "You have four words in your sentence." Counting words helped focus his writing and assisted him with conceptualizing concept-of-word. He needed to understand that our talk represented more than a stream of meaning--it contains separate words.

I gave Nick the pencil. "Say the first word in your

sentence?" Nick said "*I*" as he wrote. "What is your next word? What is the first sound that you hear at the beginning of the word *like*?" Nick wrote an *L* . "WONDERFUL! Now read what you have so far." Together we finger pointed and read, "I like." "What is your next word? What sound begins the word *to*?" Nick didn't know how to make the *t*, so I quickly wrote it for him at the top half of our book which he then copied into his sentence. "Now read what you have so far. What is your next word?"

Nick said, "*ski*". But he didn't know how to make an *s*. So again, I demonstrated and he added it to his sentence.

Then, I added, "A period or a little dot goes at the end of the sentence." Nick was not sure what I meant by end so he put the dot at the beginning. "Nick, that is the beginning or start of your sentence. The dot goes here." With this final coaching, he completed his sentence.

During the first several weeks of tutoring, I assisted Nick with letters he didn't know how to write. I always used the flip-side of his writing page for demonstration and practice. When he didn't know how to write an initial letter, I demonstrated, talking aloud about how to form the letter as I wrote. Then Nick practiced writing the letter one or two times before copying it into his sentence. I made a policy of never writing on his writing page. He was the author of his sentence.

After Nick completed his sentence, I closed his journal and rewrote his sentence correctly on a paper strip. (Closing his journal insured that he didn't focus on his own misspellings. I didn't want him to become *uptight* about spelling errors which could influence his willingness to write freely.) He read and finger-pointed to each word on the strip. Next, I took a pair of scissors, cut out each word and mixed them up on the table. "Can you put your sentence back together again?" At first, Nick had no idea how to do this. I prompted him: "Say your sentence again. What word does your sentence begin with? What is the next word? What letter does *like* begin with? Which one of the words that you have left begins with an *l*?" With my prompting, Nick put the sentence together. Then I asked, "Read your sentence again. Remember, point to each word as you read."

The sentence writing portion of the lesson helped Nick apply his rudimentary knowledge of letter formation and sounds to his writing. Moreover, rewriting the sentence on a sentence strip, cutting it apart, and putting it back together also reinforced his letter knowledge. In order to put the sentence together, he had to use what he knew about initial consonants and their sounds. Physically cutting the sentence apart, also reinforced knowledge about concept-of-word.

Over the next two weeks, our lessons followed a similar format. Nick reread three books (level 2), worked on letter recognition and production, wrote a sentence where he began to represent some of the initial consonants, and read a new book. By the end of the second week, he could recognize most of the letters. I didn't worry too much about his consistent confusion of *b* and *d*, his shaky knowledge of infrequently used letters such as *v* and *j*, or his inability to quickly name the vowels. This knowledge would come later. During these first weeks our goal was consonant recognition and production.

Introduction of a New Book

The process of introducing new books is critical to insuring the success of the child's reading. With a new book, Nick and I always examined the picture on the cover and read the title. Then we looked through the book, talking about the pictures and about what was happening on each page. I included in the discussion much of the vocabulary as we paged through the story. As we talked, I pointed to some of the difficult words. Given that many of the books had a surprise ending, we guessed what might happen and didn't look at the last page. After this preview, we would go back and begin reading the story.

When Nick was reading levels 1, 2, and 3 books, I showed him how to read most, if not all, of the book. I read the story aloud and pointed to each word. After I read a page, he would read and finger-point the same page (echo reading) until we completed the book. After the echo reading, he would read and finger-point the whole book by himself. I offered support as needed.

Program Management

I kept brief notes on each lesson so that I could quickly plan for the next day. (See the reproducible form, Early Steps Daily Log, located at the end of this chapter.) My notes included the three books we read at the beginning, a couple of comments about where we were with word study, and anything I noticed that would help with my lesson for the next day. I also recorded his sentence and made brief notes about skills taught as part of

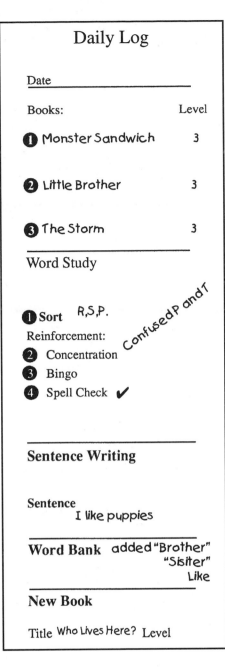

Daily Log

Date _____

Books: Level

❶ Monster Sandwich   3

❷ Little Brother   3

❸ The Storm   3
_____

Word Study

❶ Sort   R,S,P.   *Confused P and T*
Reinforcement:
❷ Concentration
❸ Bingo
❹ Spell Check ✔
_____

Sentence Writing

Sentence
      I like puppies
_____

Word Bank   added "Brother"
                        "Sister"
                         Like
_____

New Book

Title Who Lives Here? Level

the sentence writing. Finally, I wrote down the books we were reading.

After completing my notes, I planned the next day's lesson. This included selecting the books for rereading and our new book and making plans about which letters to review and teach. I kept everything in a loose-leaf notebook with pockets in the front and back for inserting the books (three old ones in the front, the new one in the back). The notebook also contained blank copies of the Early Steps Daily Log. Being prepared saved instructional time and kept our lessons flowing.

September and October

Rereading Familiar Books

By end of the first week Nick was getting into the routine of rereading familiar books. Each day I selected three level 2 or easy level 3 books that he had already read. (Having me select the books saved time). The first two books he had already read several times during previous lessons, which meant that we always started our lesson with successful reading experiences. The third book reread, he had only read once before. It was the new book introduced the previous day. On most days the third book tended to be slightly more difficult than the other two.

I wanted him to read these books quite fluently. If he needed some help getting started, I might read the first page and then let him read the rest himself. After Nick read, I pointed to three or four words in the book and asked him to read them. By the end of the third week, I moved him entirely into level three books.

Word Bank

During our second week we started a word bank. His bank consisted of individual 3 x 5 index cards which we kept in a small plastic bag inside our notebook. In the beginning his word bank had from five to seven words. I selected high frequency words which he kept meeting in the small books as well as one or two words that kept coming up in his sentence writing (*mom, dad*). Initially, I selected words that were both concrete and visually dissimilar so that they would be easy for him to discriminate and learn (*cat, mom, dad, grandmother, dog*). I wrote each of these words on separate cards and before our daily lesson, I would flash each one. We might work for several days on the same five words until he could recognize them. Then, I would send the words he knew home to read to his mom, and we would add more words to his bank. After several weeks, I began increasing the number of words in his bank to about ten words.

Letter and Picture Sorts

Now that Nick could name most of the consonants, the next step in the lesson changed to reflect his growing knowledge. By the second week, I started teaching him the initial consonant sounds through picture and letter sorts. Before starting this teaching, I organized the letter and picture cards alphabetically in a small file box so I could immediately pull out the cards for our lesson.

Nick first needed to hear the differences in letter sounds. So I carefully selected three letter sounds that looked and sounded quite different from one another. For example, I began with the phonemes /s/, /m/ and /b/ because they could easily be discriminated auditorially and visually. Nick also knew the names of these letters. Beginning with discriminable sounds and letters made the task far easier than beginning with letters much closer to one another in form and sound such as *m* and *n*, or *b*, *p*, and *d*.

42

I started with the picture cards for *m*, *b*, and *s*. Before beginning, Nick and I flipped through the cards naming the pictures. If he hesitated or did not know the name of the picture, I didn't use the card. I was teaching the beginning sounds represented by the pictures--not picture names. Pictures he did not know, I put aside and didn't use. I used twelve cards--four for each letter. Then, I placed three picture cards across the top with the rest of the cards in a pile.

My directions went something like this:

"You will listen for words that begin with the same sound. Some of the words will begin like *mouse*, *bear* or *sun*. We will read the names of these pictures and decide where they go. Watch me. I will do the first one."

I picked up the picture card *milk* and placed it under the *mouse*. Next, I pronounced both words "*Mouse, milk--milk* goes under mouse because they begin alike. Now, you do the next one."

If Nick sorted incorrectly, I corrected him. For example, when he put *ball* under the wrong column. I said, "Listen, *mouse-ball*. No, those two words do not have the beginning sound," and I moved the card into the correct column and pronounced both words. "*Bear* and *ball* have the same sound at the beginning." After each sort, Nick read the column.

Nick and I took turns sorting the pictures by beginning consonant sounds. Each time we added a picture to a column, I asked him to pronounce all of the picture words in that column

and we talked about whether the picture contained the same beginning sound as the others. We also examined how the sound felt in our mouth and lips.

I did not use more than four pictures in a column. Four pictures provide enough practice with discrimination while keeping the task simple. A complete picture sort looks like the following:

By the next day, Nick did the picture sorts for *m*, *s*, and *b* confidently as he began to hear the initial sounds. So we went to the next step--linking the sounds with the letters. I used the same picture cards, but instead, I placed the *s*, *b*, and *m* letter cards horizontally on the table and said:

"If we want to write the word *sun*, the first letter would be an *s*. The *s* stands for the first sound in *sun*. The letter *b* stands for the first sound in *ball* and the *m* says the first sound in *match*. Now let's sort these pictures under the right letter. I will do the first one. *Bird* has a *b* sound. I am going to put it here." Each time we sorted I called attention to the letter at the top.

Then, we sorted the same pictures and letters again, but this time I took the picture away directly after he placed it under

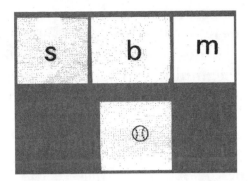

the letter. If you leave all of the pictures down under the letter, the child tends to sort to the pictures and not to the letter. I wanted to make sure he linked the initial sound with the letter rather than to pictures, so after each sort we removed the picture. I randomized the picture cards and put them in a pile. After he sorted each card under a given letter, I removed the card, leaving only the three letters. Then he sorted the next picture, and I removed the card. This forced him to match the picture with the letter.

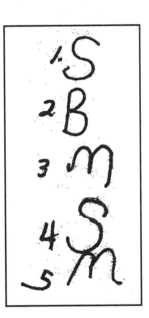

The next day, we did the letter-picture sorting task again. I then reinforced his knowledge with a spelling test. I read about six words having either the *m*, *s*, or *b* sound at the beginning and asked him to write down the first letter he heard.

The spelling task not only served to clinch these sounds, but it also demonstrated for Nick that he could begin representing these initial sounds in his writing. Once we started to do these quick spell checks, I noticed that he began to include more initial and final consonant sounds in his sentences.

After several days, Nick demonstrated a solid understanding of the *m*, *s*, or *b*. He confidently placed the pictures under the appropriate letters and wrote the initial consonants of these words in quick spell checks. We were ready to move on. So, at our next session, I dropped the *b* and added the *t*. This gave Nick two known letter sounds and only one new letter to learn. By keeping two old letters, I reinforced previous knowledge and provided him with a known base for comparing the new letter sound with the old ones. I selected *t* as the new letter because it sounded and looked different from either the *m* or *s*. I always thought about these visual-auditory factors when designing my teaching sequence and reminded myself about working from the known to the unknown.

We followed exactly the same progression with the next letters. We began first with pictures until he could hear the sounds at the beginning of the words. Already knowing the initial sounds of *m* and *s* helped him discriminate the sound of *t*.

Once he could discriminate sounds using pictures, I again put the three letter cards at the top: *m, t, s,* and he matched the initial sound of the picture names to the letters. Finally, I reinforced his knowledge with spelling where I dictated four to five words and Nick wrote down the first letter. After he could

do a three-letter sort confidently and spell them correctly in our spell checks, we moved on. I continued to drop and add a new letter so that he always had two known letters for learning and comparing initial sounds. We followed the same procedure for the remaining consonants. I didn't bother teaching him the *x, q* or *z--* given that so few first grade words begin with any of these letters.

I reinforced his knowledge of letters in other aspects of the lesson where we talked about words beginning with certain letters during reading, and I pressed him for applying letters he had worked on during sentence writing. Moreover, Nick's mother helped him at home with the alphabet. When I sent home books for Nick, I always tucked a little note inside explaining the letters that Nick needed to practice. Having such strong support at home assisted him enormously.

Even so, Nick took about six weeks to progress through the consonants. He progressed more slowly than many other students in the program because of his attention difficulties. Some days he struggled to focus on anything, which made remembering certain letters from one day to the next extra challenging. We constantly reviewed until he knew them. When he couldn't remember how to write a letter in his sentence, I made a note of it and would reteach it the following day.

The important thing to keep in mind is that the child directs your progress. Often we teachers have a tendency to move children too quickly before knowledge is consolidated. We want to get on with it! Yet, letter knowledge and a rudimentary understanding about the sounds represented by initial consonants becomes the foundation for the next phases of word study. Without it, the child won't make much progress. So, spending time here was important for Nick.

Before moving on, let's take a moment to summarize what we have done so far with teaching the letters and initial sounds:

- picture sorting--discriminating sounds using only pictures; two known sounds with one unknown
- letter-picture sorting
- spelling checks
- Repeating the sequence with another set of three letters--two known, one unknown.

An informal assessment provides instant information about whether or not a child is ready to move from the letter to the word sorts. Over a two-day span, I asked Nick to name and write the alphabet and take a spelling test. For this informal assessment, I simply read off words representing the initial consonant sounds and asked him to write the first letter. He confidently named all of the letters with the exception of confusing *b* and *d* and only made three errors on the spell check. I took notes about these confusions for reteaching over the next several days as we progressed into word families.

Sentence Writing

During this five-week time period, Nick became more confident in his sentence writing. Initially his sentences looked like a random string of letters with no spaces between the words. This gradually changed as he gained a better understanding of how to do the task and as he learned more about consonants and initial sounds.

After coming up with the sentence, I insisted that Nick repeat it while counting the number of words on his fingers. It took about a week of reminding him to repeat and count before he began doing it by himself. He also worked on putting a finger space between each word as he wrote. All of these procedures gave him strategies for writing his own sentence and facilitated his conceptual understanding of wordness.

It is important to understand that sentence writing can also be quite a challenging task for a teacher. You have to be constantly thinking about what to push for. This means keeping in mind what the child knows, or is on the verge of knowing, and what is beyond the child's current stage of development. Always try to find something in the sentence writing to teach which the child can succeed in learning. Then, push, but don't push beyond what the child can do and always think about ways for the child to begin using strategies himself. The art of this teaching is the turning of strategy knowledge over to the child.

For example, during the first week of October, Nick wrote: *I play soccer on the playground.* He forgot how to write *I*. We had just read a book where sentences beginning with *I* made up the pattern carried throughout the book. I quickly picked up the book from the table and said, "Nick, I think you can figure out how to spell the word *I*. Reread the first page of this book." That was all it took for Nick to write *I* on his paper.

He did not know how to write the *p* in *play*. We hadn't gotten to *p* yet in our letter sort tasks, so I simply wrote it in the work area of his sentence book, and he copied it in. I knew he couldn't get it so there was no point frustrating him. He wasn't there yet! But, he did know how to write the *s* in *soccer*. After he wrote down the *s*, I decided to push for the *r*. We had just done the *r* in our letter sorts, and I thought he could manage it. I made two sound boxes in our work area and wrote the *s* in the first box and said, "You got the first letter in *soccer* perfectly. Now I am going to challenge you. I think you might be able to get the last sound in *soccer*. Say, *soccer*. What sound do you hear in this last box?" Nick, wrote an *r* in the box and then copied it into his sentence. I ended up giving him the *o* in *on*. Normally, at this stage I wouldn't have bothered doing this because we were a way from thinking about vowels, but he knew something was missing at the beginning. So, I wrote the word *on* for him in the work area which he inserted into his sentence, and we continued.

He had no idea how to write the next word, *the*, but it happened to be one of his word bank words. I quickly pulled out the card. "Nick, what is this word?" He said, *"the"* and then used the card for copying the word into his sentence.

In a matter of minutes, I used several different procedures to assist Nick in meeting his own challenges. He used a book, his word bank, and sound boxes. Always in the back of my mind is the question: What does Nick know or just about know that he can use for figuring something out for himself? This is what I mean by art! Teaching as art doesn't happen over night. So, be patient with yourself!

Introducing a new book

The teacher must be planful in selecting a new book. It can be neither too hard nor too easy. Books must be challenging enough for children to learn something, but not too difficult. Books that are too difficult won't work and will only frustrate the child. In fact, books can't be classified as easy or hard; they can only be designated that way in relation to the reader. A good rule of thumb for deciding about book difficulty is the percentage of errors the child makes while reading. A book is too difficult if, after book introduction and guidance, a child reads less than 90% of the words accurately.

Before the lesson, I spent several minutes choosing a book which I felt would be appropriate for Nick. Yet, I always remained opened to changing my mind as our lesson progressed. My final selection also depended on his attitude. If Nick seemed out-of-sorts during our lesson in situations where I might have pushed too hard, or if he seemed extra tired, I would switch from my original choice to an easier book. Some days he simply needed an ego-boost! Or, if our lesson was going well with Nick thriving on challenges, at the last moment, I might change to a slightly more difficult new book.

Nick and I also felt comfortable about abandoning a book mid-stream when it ended up being too difficult. After reading several pages together and feeling Nick's frustration, I would switch to another book that worked better. "Nick, this book seems too hard for you right now. Let's wait a few weeks and try it again."

After having a few such false starts, Nick also began to take some responsibility about making decisions to abandon books. "I don't want to read this book. It has too many hard words!" Such open talk about book difficulty went far beyond our daily lessons. Nick was learning tools for selecting books on his own.

The goal for this part of the lesson is gradually to push the child to more challenging books, but to do it in a way that the child hardly notices what is happening. In these early stages, I supplied more support than later in the year when Nick began to read more independently. Throughout the lesson I continually prompted him to use strategies while teaching him ways to solve his own reading challenges.

Let's take a moment to summarize book introduction strategies for this early emergent level (book levels 1-4):

1. Story Introduction and Picture Walk

The goal with story introduction is to provide enough support so that the child becomes familiar with the story line and vocabulary. We want the child to feel confident about reading the story before he begins.

- Talk about the title and make predictions about what the story will be about.
- Go through the story, page by page, reserving the last two or three pages, particularly if the story line contains a twist at the end.
- As you page through the book, talk about what is happening on each page using the vocabulary on the pages. Point to some of the words which the child might not know as you talk. In this way the reader will be familiar with the vocabulary before reading.

2. First Reading

Provide enough support in the first reading for the child to begin reading it on his own. Begin with the title. Read and finger-point it. Have him do the same thing. Then begin reading and finger pointing the first one or two pages until the predictability of the book allows the child to take over.

- Read aloud the first several pages. Point to the words as you read.
- After you read a page, ask him to read it (echo read).
- Point to each word as you model. Then tell him to read it with his finger.
- You read a page; the child reads the page. Continue echo reading until he begins to get the pattern and starts reading it on his own.
- Only support him until he can take over.

3. Learning Strategies

During the reading, constantly think about ways for the child to become aware of strategies. At this early emergent level, use strategies based on what the reader already knows or is on the verge of learning.

For example, Nick knew most of the beginning letter sounds, knew that pictures supported the story line, and had some experience with predictable story patterns. When coming to a word he didn't know, I prompted him to use this knowledge to problem solve. My prompting often went like this:

- Look at the first letter. Use that first letter to help you.
- What does the word start with?
- Read this line. Skip that hard word. Now let's read it again. What makes sense in the sentence?
- Look at the picture. What word goes with the picture?
- You have read this word before. Let's go back and find it on the page you just read.

Once Nick figured out a word, I often went back and reinforced his recognition with prompts similar to these:

- How did you know the word is_____?
- How many times on these two pages do you find the word_____?

Home-school Partnerships

After about three weeks, I invited Nick's mother and dad to observe a lesson. Afterwards we talked about how Nick was progressing and things that they might do at home. We decided that Nick would take his sentence home each day, put it together and read it again. He would also take home one or two books that we had read in our lessons. (Sometimes he ended up reading them to his cat—this was fine, too.) Having him reread books at home not only gave him extra practice, but it also gave Nick an opportunity to show his parents how well he was doing. Their encouragement helped Nick's progress.

The following guidelines might help:

1. **Initial parent contact**. Before the first tutoring session, call the parents. In this conversation explain the Early Steps

Program. Talk about key features of the program:

- early intervention
- designed to accelerate performance of first grader
- includes a balanced approach to reading (reading, phonics, writing)
- thirty minutes per day of one-to-one tutoring

Explain that their child will progress more rapidly with home support. Tell them that you will call in a few weeks so they can observe a lesson.

2. **Plan a parent visit.** After about two weeks of tutoring, invite parents to observe a session. If possible arrange for ten minutes after the session to talk about the child and the program. Help parents assist the child at home. Give an information sheet, located at the end of this chapter to the parent.

3. **Parent Information Sheet**. At the end of this chapter are two parent information sheets, one for a girl and the other for a boy (Family support in the Early Steps Program). These copy pages contain guidelines for helping parents assist the child at home. Give parents a copy of the appropriate information sheet during your first parent conference.

4. **Keeping in touch.** Call once a month to share the progress you see.

Closing Comments

By the end of our first five weeks together, I took time to reflect about Nick's progress. When immersed in day-to-day teaching, it sometimes feels like progress is painfully slow. Some days, it seemed like we went backwards as I would reteach something that he knew the week before. Yet, when reviewing my notes, I realized how much Nick now knew about reading. He had about 15 words in his word bank, knew all of his letters, and practically all of his consonant sounds. Moreover, he was beginning to use initial consonant sounds as a strategy for figuring out unknown words, for writing sentences, and for doing picture and letter sorts. He was even beginning to use some final consonant sounds in his writing. He now had the foundation to become a reader!

DAILY LOG

Date _____

Books: Level

❶

❷

❸

_____
Word Study

❶ **Sort**
Reinforcement:
❷ Concentration
❸ Bingo
❹ Spell Check

_____
Sentence Writing

Sentence

_____
Word Bank

_____
New Book

Title   Level

Date _____

Books: Level

❶

❷

❸

_____
Word Study

❶ **Sort**
Reinforcement:
❷ Concentration
❸ Bingo
❹ Spell Check

_____
Sentence Writing

Sentence

_____
Word Bank

_____
New Book

Title   Level

FAMILY SUPPORT IN THE EARLY STEPS PROGRAM

Each day, I will send a book home with your child. I would like for her to read it to you. In addition, I will also send home the cut-up sentence in case she wants to put it together again.

A BOOK EVERY DAY!

Sit beside her. Remind her to point to each word as she reads. This will help her focus on each word as she reads.

Let her try to figure out some of the words herself—particularly words that are phonetically regular. If she comes to a word she can't figure out, wait a moment. Coach her with some questions: "How can you figure this word out yourself? What word makes sense here? Look at the first letter. Does the first letter help you?" Wait about five seconds before telling her the word.

If your child is having difficulty reading the book, do echo reading. You read a page. Then let her read the same page.

Compliment her. "I loved the way you figured out that word all by yourself. I am so proud of how you are reading".
Other positive behaviors to notice:

- pointing to each word as she says it
- self-correcting any word errors
- reading books on her own
- reading books to younger brothers and sisters or to pets (stuffed or real)

If the book is too hard, abandon it. We don't want her to become discouraged. If she has difficulty reading more than five words out of a hundred, the book is too difficult.

THE CUT-UP SENTENCE

Your child might want to put together the sentence we worked on today. Watch her put the sentence together and read it. If the words are not in the right order, let her read it to discover how to put it together differently. Guide with comments:

- How does this word begin?
- Does this word make sense here?
- Look at the word again. What is the first letter?

PREPARING FOR TOMORROW

Put the book back into the ziplock bag and then into her school bag so that I can send another book home tomorrow. Please feel free to call me if you have any questions.

Telephone_____
Name_____

FAMILY SUPPORT IN THE EARLY STEPS PROGRAM

Each day, I will send a book home with your child. I would like for him to read it to you. In addition, I will also send home the cut-up sentence in case he wants to put it together again.

A BOOK EVERY DAY!

Sit beside him. Remind him to point to each word as he reads. This will help him focus on each word as he reads.

Let him try to figure out some of the words himself—particularly words that are phonetically regular. If he comes to a word he can't figure out, wait a moment. Coach him with some questions: "How can you figure this word out yourself? What word makes sense here? Look at the first letter. Does the first letter help you?" Wait about five seconds before telling him the word.

If your child is having difficulty reading the book, do echo reading. You read a page. Then let him read the same page.

Compliment him. "I loved the way you figured out that word all by yourself. I am so proud of how you are reading".

Other positive behaviors to notice:

- pointing to each word as he says it
- self-correcting any word errors
- reading books on his own
- reading books to younger brothers and sisters or to pets (stuffed or real)

If the book is too hard, abandon it. We don't want him to become discouraged. If he has difficulty reading more than five words out of a hundred, the book is too difficult.

THE CUT-UP SENTENCE

Your child might want to put together the sentence we worked on today. Watch him put the sentence together and read it. If the words are not in the right order, let him read it to discover how to put it together differently. Guide with comments:

- How does this word begin?
- Does this word make sense here?
- Look at the word again. What is the first letter?

PREPARING FOR TOMORROW

Put the book back into the ziplock bag and then into his school bag so that I can send another book home tomorrow. Please feel free to call me if you have any questions.

Telephone_____

Name_____

Chapter 4
Winter

As Nick and I moved into the winter months, he continued to make slow, steady progress. By December, he was well settled into school. The routine of our lessons, the support at home, and the coordination of instruction with the classroom moved him along.

Coordinated Instruction

It makes sense that children like Nick progress more quickly in special reading programs when classroom and tutorial instruction rest on a similar instructional philosophy. My district insured that such coordination took place by involving as many teachers in Early Steps as possible. By the end of three years of implementation, every Title One and first grade teacher in our district had participated in the Early Steps program. By the end of year four, most kindergarten, grade two, and resource teachers had taken the graduate class and had tutored at least one child. With so many teachers owning the program, we could guarantee more cohesive instruction within the classroom, in resource rooms, and in the Title One Program.

Teachers began adapting Early Steps strategies within the regular classroom. Even though the last chapter of this book (Chapter 6) contains a detailed description of ways to implement Early Steps in the classroom, let's take a brief look at Nick's classroom instruction to see why I was not the only one responsible for his progress. Nick's teacher, Marilyn, also tutored a child in Early Steps and, therefore, understood how the program operated with individual children. With this knowledge, she incorporated Early Steps within the larger context of her classroom.

Nick's Classroom. All of Marilyn's students participated in sentence writing, word sorting, and small group guided reading lessons. Her students did sentence writing as a whole group activity. Each had a sentence book and wrote each day about an individual experience. Marilyn taught them how to say the sentences as they wrote and to feel comfortable spelling using the sounds and letters they knew.

She did picture, letter, and word sorts as part of large and small group instruction. Most word sorting activities occurred as part of small group lessons. She also reinforced word sort knowledge with spelling activities.

For small group guided reading lessons, she and three other adults taught simultaneously in her classroom. The adults were parents and Title One tutors, who led groups five days per week. Each adult worked with four to five children reading on approximately the same level. The small groups read from old basals, sets of small books, and multiple copies of trade books organized by increasing levels of difficulty.

In addition, Marilyn's first graders had from 20 to 30 minutes each day for individual reading from an in-class library of books organized into plastic bins according to difficulty level. Each child kept a portfolio containing a checklist of books read. She also expected the children to read at home as part of a district-wide home reading program.

Reflections about Nick

Marilyn and I talked frequently about Nick's progress. As we examined where Nick was with Early Steps during these winter months, we reminded ourselves that children progress differently. Some progress more quickly than others. A child might move along consistently for a while and then seem to go for several weeks with little discernible progress. Then, they will spurt ahead. We can't compare one child's performance with another.

When Nick and I looked back through his writing and at the books read earlier in the fall, we saw proof of wonderful progress. So take time periodically for returning to earlier work and seeing just how far you have come. What a sense of satisfaction for a child to see for himself how much he has learned!

Winter Progress

Rereading familiar Books

By December and January Nick was well into level four and five books. I began with the more patterned books in these levels and then advanced to level five and six books which became progressively less patterned. Nick could no longer rely so much on predictable text and his keen memory for the words on the page. Often children will crash a bit with less patterned books. Nick was no exception. He had to attend more closely to individual words and rely more on sight words. The word bank became critical to his transition.

Word bank. At the beginning of the lesson, we went through the words in his bank. If he could remember a word for three or four days in a row, he took it home. Each day we tried to add one or two additional words from the books he was rereading. I selected words which occurred frequently in the books. Some days we didn't add any words depending on how well Nick read words already in his bank.

It is important to understand that this word bank may be quite different from those children might have used where the number of words in the bank grew in size throughout the year. This bank is not a growing collection or a record of the words the child knows. Instead, it remains quite small--never more than about 20 words, and it always changes. Once a child consistently knows a word, remove it. Give the child the word to take home and add another. Or, if the child is having difficulty reading the words in the bank, reduce the number of words until the child succeeds in reading all of them.

Wait-time. With book reading, the most challenging task for the teacher is wait-time. As Nick reread the three familiar books at the beginning of the lesson and came to a word he didn't know, I made many small, but important decisions. I could jump in and tell him the word, coach him through it, or simply sit back and let him figure it out on his own. If Nick never had opportunities to correct his own errors, he would have little chance of employing strategies essential for independence. We teachers tend to leap in too quickly, to take over, and not let the child work through his own reading challenges. Yet, I didn't want Nick to struggle endlessly and become discouraged. Sluggish reading also contributes to poor comprehension. So here are some questions I ask myself when making decisions about jumping in or waiting:

1. Is the word decodable, taking into consideration the child's current knowledge?

Some words such as *caught* and *where* are practically impossible for any first grader to figure out. If you know the word is beyond where the child is, tell him. Don't let the child struggle.

2. Can the child figure it out based on his own stage of word study? If so, coach him through it using prompts:

- Read the line again. What does the word start with?
- Look, we just did these patterns in our word sorts. (Quickly pull out the word sort cards displaying the pattern.) Read these through quickly. Now look. Does this word have the same pattern? See if you can read it now.
- I think you might have that word in your word bank. Let's see if we can find it.
- We had this same word in another book we just read. Find the page in the book and have the child read it. What is this word? Is it the same word you are working on?

Once you have gone through these questions a few times, challenge the child to use strategies on his own. "How do you think you might figure out that word? What can you do all by yourself?"

Another issue is finger-pointing. Many children at this time of year want to give it up, but don't let them. Finger-pointing helps them focus attention on individual words on the page. Also, let the child do his own finger-pointing. Sometimes, when Nick forgot or didn't want to use his finger for reading, I caught myself doing the finger-pointing for him. Don't take over. So, even when the child balks at the idea of finger reading, hold him to it, explaining that it will help him read. For it to work, he has to do it himself!

Word Study

By December Nick began the short *a* word families. We started with the simplest word patterns (*hat*, *cat* and *map*) and then progressed to more advanced patterns (short *i, o, u* and *e*).

The word families extend upon initial consonant knowledge introduced to Nick earlier with the picture and letter sorting. With word families only the initial consonant sound differs, which forces the child to understand how initial consonants (onsets) operate within words. Each word family has the same vowel-consonant (rime) which also directs the child's attention to the short vowel-consonant patterns. (See the word sort chart at the conclusion of this chapter.)

I began with three patterns using four words in each pattern and selected twelve words, four in each group, that had the simplest configurations. For example, I did not use any that began with blends (*cat*, *fat*, etc. rather than *flat*). The three words across the top must be known words so the child can work from the known to the unknown. So before beginning the word

sort, I taught Nick the words *cat*, *fan*, and *cap*. To make it easier, I drew little pictures on the cards so that he could immediately recognize them. Then, I placed the three cards horizontally on the table and put the remaining cards in a pile and said, " I can put these words under *cat*, under *fan* or under *cap*. Watch. I'll do the first one." I picked up the word *man* and placed it in the *fan* column and read, *man* and *fan*. "You try the next one."

Then, Nick picked up the word *hat* and placed it under *cap*. I said, "I don't think the *cap* column is the best place for *hat*. I think *hat* looks more like *cat*. Put it here and let's read it together--*cat*, *hat*. Yes, that works better. *Cat* and *hat* look and sound similar." I didn't offer any more explanation than this. Nick needed to see for himself how the word patterns operated. As we took turns sorting the words, Nick began to get the idea. After each sort, he read the words in the column. The known word at the top (header) supported him in reading the other three words in the column.

The teaching sequence is the same for all of the word sorts. Always have the child place the word card under the header. Then ask the child to read the column. Sorting the words first provides support for the reading. Our first word sort looked something like this:

cat	fan	cap
hat	man	map
mat	pan	sap
pat	can	tap

Notice that it is the final consonant that actually lets the child know which word belongs in a column. Not only must children pay attention to the initial consonant as they read the words, but they also must attend to the final consonant. This helps the child extend earlier knowledge of initial consonants to another part of the word.

The next day, I used the same twelve words and headers. I started by placing the header words (*cat*, *fan* and *cap*) on the

table for him to read. (Remember, word sorting doesn't work unless the child knows the headers.) He took the word set used the previous day and sorted them one by one. After placing each word, he read the top word and the words placed below it.

During these introductory lessons with a particular word sort, I did not explain why a word goes in a particular category. At first, such explanations are wasted effort. They fall on deaf ears. Teacher explanations make little sense until the child has made some of his own discoveries. Hold off until the child has worked with a word sort successfully for a number of days. Then ask some leading questions to assist the reader in verbalizing discoveries. Some helpful questions are: "What do you notice about all of the words in this column?" "Why doesn't this word fit here?"

Reinforcement activities. After about a week, Nick had the idea of the *at*, *ap* and *an* families. He could sort the words into the columns, but he was still a bit hesitant with some words. He could do it, but not fluently. To reinforce his understanding, we played the game concentration. We used 12 cards, four for each family and mixed them up. Then, I laid them face down on the table, and the game began. Nick turned over two cards, read the words and noted if they came from the same family. If they matched (came from the same family), he kept the cards and took another turn. If they didn't, he turned both cards over, and I took a turn. The person with the most cards at the end wins the game.

Concentration helps students internalize word patterns. The child must read the words randomly and hold a word pattern in memory while looking for a match. Besides that, it broke the word sort routine. Nick loved the competition and for some reason, his memory always seemed a bit sharper than mine!

Spelling is the second way to reinforce word pattern knowledge. Again, spelling activities work best after the child has some idea of the word pattern being sorted. After Nick had sorted the words correctly several times, I reinforced his understanding with a brief three to four word spelling test. After completing the sort, we did quick spelling checks using the back side of a writing page in his sentence book. At first, Nick spelled words in just one family.

Over the next several days he spelled words in the *an* and *ap* families. Finally, I had him spell a random list of words representing all three families.

It took about a month for Nick to gain proficiency with the short *a* families. During this month I also added words to the sorts which contained some initial consonant clusters (*clap, flat, plan*). Once a child feels comfortable sorting the easiest words in a sort, those that have the simplest letter configurations (CVC), gradually add more complex words such as those with initial blends and consonant digraphs (*th, sh, ch*). I slipped in the blends and digraphs with all the word pattern sorts. In this way, the child learns them gradually and painlessly as part of the word sort routine.

Now that Nick could sort, read, and spell words in the *cat*, *can*, and *cap* families, it was time to move on and add the *sack* family. Again, we only sorted three word patterns at a time. I always kept two old families when adding a new one so he could use known knowledge to support him in learning the new. Given that Nick knew the *man*, *hat*, and *map* families, each day I dropped one of these three and added the *back* word family. This also meant that we constantly reviewed at least two of the three old families while learning the new.

hat	can	sack
cat	van	tack
mat	plan	back
flat	tan	rack

We continued sorting the *hat*, *man*, and *back* families, including words with blends (*black, track*) until he could sort, read, and spell them.

Changing Word Sorts. Now that Nick could sort the words easily, play concentration quite effortlessly, and spell the words when presented in mixed patterns, I evaluated whether or not he was ready to progress from the short *a* families to the next pattern, the short *i* families. My evaluation involved asking him to read the words as I randomly presented him the cards. Given that he succeeded in reading them all, I felt confident about advancing to the short *i* families.

I didn't advance Nick to the next pattern until he demonstrated solid understanding of the short *a* families. Solid understanding, particularly of the first word sort is vital to a child's progress. Sometimes, we tend to move a child along faster than we should. The first word sort takes far longer than the remaining ones. Be patient. Remind yourself that it is far better to spend too much time on a skill than move through it too quickly. With Nick, I wanted him to feel completely secure with the short *a* families before moving on. He needed this knowledge as a foundation for the work that followed. Remember, we always move from the known to the unknown. If the known is not firm, then further progress will be difficult.

Short *i* families. By January we started the *i* families. We dropped for the moment all of the *a* families and moved completely into the *i*'s (see the word families chart at the end of this chapter). The sequence was identical to that already

pig	**sit**	**win**
fig	**kit**	**pin**
dig	**fit**	**fin**
wig	**pit**	**tin**

described. I taught him three header words: *pig, sit, win*. He sorted the three families over about a week's time. Each day I would add a few different words to the sort. Then I began reinforcing knowledge through spell checks and concentration. Again, we started by spelling words in one pattern and progressed to spelling across patterns. As he became more proficient, I added words to the sorts containing consonant blends and digraphs (*spin, chin, grin, twig*).

Next, I added the *kick* pattern. For the next several days, we dropped one of the *i* family word patterns (*pig, sit, win*) and added the *kick* family words. Then, I measured his proficiency with the short *i* families by once again asking him to read the word cards as I presented them randomly. He read most with ease--we could move on.

Combining the *a* and *i* patterns. Before beginning the short *o* families we spent several days combining the *a* and *i* words groups into one sort. Combining two vowel families into one sort is a critical transition step. This single sort with two different vowels brings vowel discrimination into play for the first time with words that the child already knows. We spent several days working with the *cat*, *pig*, and *back* families and then with the *pig*, *win*, and *lap* families.

pig	**cat**	**win**
fig	**mat**	**pin**
dig	**fat**	**fin**
wig	**sat**	**tin**

Reinforcement activities stressed spelling and concentration. Initially, Nick confused some of the *i*'s and *a*'s, but by the end of the week, he discriminated them quite readily. This work prepares the child for the short vowel pattern work that comes later in the year.

Word Sort Decisions. After mastering the short *a* and *i* word families, I introduced the short *o* patterns. After about a week, Nick did them perfectly. At this point, I had an important decision to make. Should I go through the *e* and *u* families or should I skip them and move directly to the short vowel patterns?

Morris (1992) explains that the decision depends on how quickly and firmly the child has internalized the patterns so far. After sorting the three short vowel families, most children have become quite adept with ending consonants, rhyming words, and with beginning consonant substitutions. Moreover, they have also acquired a substantial number of short vowel words as part of their sight vocabulary. If a child has moved through the short *a*, *i* and *o* families fairly effortlessly, then skip ahead to the short vowel sorts. Don't do the *e* and *u* word family sorts. The child will have plenty of practice with these elements with the next set of word sorts. But, if the child has progressed very slowly, acquiring this knowledge with some difficulty, go ahead and do the *e* and *u* families. Most children, even those who have needed more time with the previous sorts, will move quickly through these last word families. In any case, remember with each word group to follow the established procedure:

- The child must know the three header words.
- The first time through the tutor and child take turns unless the child can immediately take over. The tutor supports only as needed.
- After placing the word in the column, the child reads the column.
- The following day or days after the child is becoming more automatic with a sort, reinforcement occurs through spelling and concentration.
- The child can move to the next word sort once he can read a randomized presentation of the words.

You will find a summary of the sequence for presenting word sorts on a handout, Word Sort Sequence, at the end of the chapter. Many teachers find it helpful to keep a copy of the summary handy for easy reference. After teaching Early Steps with one or two children, this sequence and the decisions that you make along the way will become so much a part of your teaching that you will no longer need to refer to it.

Sentence Writing

Laying Ground Rules. On most days Nick readily generated a sentence. However, this part of the lesson can become taxing both for the teacher and the child. Sometimes children don't know what to write or they write safe sentences where they aren't really learning anything new. They only write sentences that they know how to write. After a child writes several sentences beginning with "I love... or I like...." prod for more variability. As children become more and more comfortable, they may also want to take over the lesson. The best plan is to lay some ground rules and stick to them. My rules for Nick were as follows:

- Come prepared to our session with a sentence.
- Your sentence has to be at least five words.
- You can't start your sentence with "I like...". We have done that one enough!
- Repeat the sentence before you write.
- Say the words as you write them.
- I get to write the sentence on the sentence strip. That's the teacher's job!
- You get to reread your sentence on the strip before I cut it apart.
- I cut the sentence apart.
- You get to put it back together again and read it once more.
- You get to take your sentence home and read it to your mom.

Establishing some rules saves time and makes this portion of the lesson run more smoothly. Don't let sentence writing drag-on unnecessarily. It shouldn't take more than about seven to eight minutes.

Before moving to a discussion about Nick's writing progress, we need to examine in more detail theoretical principles regarding children's development as spellers and writers. Having this conceptual understanding at your fingertips is critical for making decisions about what to teach during sentence writing.

Developmental Spelling

We all know that spelling development is not an all-or-none process. It is fascinating to observe children as they experiment with language and to note how their early writing contains spelling errors that are very interesting. Their errors are smart and predictable. They are principled, not random. Spelling provides a window on what a child knows and offers insight about what a child needs.

Children will be at different stages within a sequential continuum. An understanding of this progression and where an individual child fits within this developmental stream is critical. Even though the stages described below are continuous rather than discrete, they can be loosely classified according to the following stages: *Preliterate*, *Semi-phonetic*, *Phonetic*, and *Transitional*.

Stage 1: Preliterate Writing

Two year old children become fascinated with using pencils and crayons for scribbling. Gradually children's drawings change with the additions of diagonals and circles to their *writing*. As they scribble grocery lists and stories, they proceed to *read* their writing to you. Children soon ask for help with letters, particularly with writing their name--the most important word of all. The child's efforts are, of course, not perfect with letters written out of sequence and in a variety of directions across the page.

Some children during these pre-school years will progress beyond copying letters to using letters to represent what they want to say. This does not happen unless children have had considerable experience being read to and assistance with letters from older children and adults. Usually these early inventions are combinations of scribbles, letters, and numbers. As children continue to experiment, these combinations become strings of letters which one can actually read.

Stage 2: Semi-phonetic

By the time children reach the semi-phonetic stage, they have a fully developed concept-of-word, and their spelling is characterized by letter-name spelling. Children in this stage use an alphabetical principle of writing to represent one syllable words and use letter name spelling in a consistent and predictable way (Read, 1975). Their writing represents direct letter-to-sound matches. The names of many consonants are actually close to the letter sounds. Therefore, children represent them quite directly. *(bk=back, ft=fat)*.

Stage 3: Phonetic

Children start to add some vowels beginning with long sounds because the letter names are equivalent matches to the sounds *(bot=boat,cak=cake)*. They also represent short vowels by the letter name which most closely approximates the sound of the letter. For example, the first short vowel to emerge correctly in children's spelling is usually the *a*. This happens because the name of the letter *a* is a closer approximation to the short sound *(man=man)* than any of the other vowels. However, substitutions routinely occur with the other short vowels (Henderson, 1990).

The other short vowels are more confusable. For example, Short *e* sounds the closest to the pronunciation of the letter *a*. So when children attempt to write words with short *e* they will typically substitute the letter *a* *(pet=pat)*. Moreover, the short *i* sound is closest to the *e* letter name. Given that there is no exact letter name which says the short *i* sound, children again select the letter name which most closely approximates it. They consistently substitute the letter *e* for short *i* *(mit=met)*. Similarly, when writing words with short *o* *(hot)*, the closest letter name is *i* *(hit)*, and the closest approximation to short *u* is *o* *(nut=not)*.

> man=man
> mit=met
> hot=hit
> nut=not

In addition to these vowel substitutions, children during this developmental period consistently omit *m* and *n* before a final consonant *(lamp=lap, friend=fred)*. The *m* and *n* are not prominent enough to stand alone because their sounds when pronounced in these word configurations are collapsed into the vowels. Therefore, children at this stage of development don't bother with them in their writing. As Henderson says, children have a natural sensitivity to use the principle of economy in their writing. If they can't hear them prominently, most won't include these sounds in their writing. These more fine tuned sound patterns emerge later in the child's development.

Stage 4: Transitional

With extensive opportunities for reading and writing, achieving first graders move into the transitional stage of spelling usually by the spring of grade one. They start representing the short vowels correctly as well as many of the long vowel patterns such as the *ai* in *pail* and the *c-v-c* silent *e* pattern (*cake*).

An understanding of developmental spelling helps us realize why children need many opportunities to explore language through writing and spelling. Spelling and the development of phonics are complementary processes. When children write the sounds that they hear, they begin to internalize the speech sounds of print. Moreover, we gain rich insights into the child's progression toward understanding the conventions of language by examining his development as a writer.

This work also provides insight about what to teach in sentence writing. We push for word elements which are within range of the child's spelling development. If a child is only representing the first and last letters of a word (*pt* for *part*), it makes no sense to push for the *ar*.

Teaching decisions. Knowledge about the developmental stages of spelling helped me make teaching decisions. I only selected one or two things to teach. Nick could only stand so much, and I wanted to keep this part of the lesson from dragging. What I taught changed according to his stage of spelling development.

Given his semi-phonetic developmental level for the first month, my teaching focused on initial and then later on both initial and final consonants in selected words. He was in the midst of learning consonant sounds through picture sorting, so pushing these same elements in his writing only served to extend his knowledge of consonant sounds.

At this stage, I obviously didn't push for short vowels. Long vowels, however, were a different story for Nick. Because of his increasing proficiency in using letter names to represent most sounds, he started to include some medial long vowels in words (*same=sam*).

In early November, Nick wrote, *I made a snow hill with my dad*. Initially he wrote: *I md a s hl w mi dd*. Given that he did so well in representing all of the important initial and final consonants, I decided to see if he could apply his letter naming strategy to medial and final long vowel sounds. For the

word, *made*, I drew three boxes, leaving the middle one blank.

"What do you hear in the middle of the word *made*?" Nick wrote in the *a*, which he then fixed in his sentence. Next, I pushed for the final *o* in *snow*. I made two boxes, putting the *s* in the first. "What do hear at the end of *snow*?" He succeeded again.

I also directly taught some common words. Notice that Nick has the word *my* correctly written, and that I wrote it on the work page above his sentence. I ended up just giving him this word. Initially he had written *mi* which is of course an excellent representation of the word. Even so, there are some small words that children use so frequently in their writing and reading that it makes sense for them to learn how to write correctly. In this instance, I said, "Nick, you see the word, *my* so often in your reading and writing. You did a wonderful job of spelling it, but big people spell it like this." Nick then erased the *mi* and replaced it with *my*.

By mid December, Nick's sentence writing clearly placed him within the phonetic stage of development. He consistently represented initial and final consonants, some initial blends as well as some long vowels. He was beginning to hear short

71

vowels in words and spell some vowels sporadically. Our work with short *a* families facilitated his advancing knowledge. Now that Nick had become quite adept with the first pattern of word family sorts (*man, cat, map, back*), I began encouraging him to apply what he was learning in word sorting to his writing.

The third week of December he wrote the sentence: *My friend Mat is coming over.* He initially wrote *Mat* as *MT*. A

my fRND Mat is Keming

OVR

quick reminder was all it took for Nick to fix the word. I pulled out the header cards for the word sorts: *cat, man, pan* and said, "What do you know about the words, *mat*? Which header would *mat* fit under?" He wrote *Mat* perfectly into his sentence. Then, I asked a leading question:

"Nick, you wrote *Mat* perfectly. How did you figure it out?", "I just looked at *cat*. *Mat* looks the same. Then I did it here."

Think about what Nick and I just did. The art of this teaching is assisting the reader in making his own connections. Always in the back of my head are the questions: How can I lead the child to apply what he knows for solving his own problems? How can I help him become more aware of his successful strategies? In this case, my questioning helped Nick link knowledge gained from word sorting to solving a spelling problem. My questioning also helped him see what he had done. Opportunities for such metacognitive reflection give ownership for learning to the child.

Before moving on, I want to make some further comments about this example. When Nick came to the word *coming* in his sentence, he asked for help. I used a couple of strategies. First, I broke the word into syllables and had him work on one syllable at a time. "Nick, the word *coming* has two parts. Let's just do the first part." He wrote *kem*. I decided not to touch the *e*. In fact, I was delighted that he heard something in the middle and an *e* actually make sense as a place holder. It would not have done any good for me to correct it. We hadn't worked with short *o* and *e* yet in the word sorts. So I accepted it. Second, I just gave him the *ing*. "Nick, the last part of the word is *ing*. We see this *ing* a lot in words. You spell it like this." With that he added the *ing* on *keming*.

72

Finally, when coaching the child to write a multi-syllable word, break the word down and do each part sequentially. Use sound boxes as needed to help the child stretch the word out and hear specific sounds. Notice in Nick's sentence, I helped him hear the *v* by taking apart the word *over*. Nick originally wrote *or*. We focused on one syllable at a time and with the help of the sound boxes, he had no difficulty adding the *v*.

Let's summarize some teaching principles gleaned from the discussion of these example sentences:

• Always consider where the child is developmentally in spelling. Don't ask the child to produce beyond his developmental level. Instead, push for what is there, or just barely beyond where the child is. Always think ahead to where the child is going and nudge him along in a developmental and logical way. If you haven't taught the short *u* yet, don't bother pushing for it in the child's writing.

• Use what you have taught in word sorts as a guide for what to pull out of the writing.

• With multi-syllable words, break the word apart and ask the child to spell each part.

• Use sound boxes to help the child stretch the word out and visually see where letters go. Remember that each space represents one phoneme. So, if you are focusing on *sh* in *ship*, you would make the sound boxes like this:

• Give children common words (*my, the*) and endings that occur frequently (*ing*) in their reading and writing.

• When the child figures something out on his own, compliment him. Ask him to tell how he did it. Always think about ways for the child to become more aware of successful strategies.

Cutting-apart the Sentence. It is about this time when children begin reading level 5 and 6 books, that we stop cutting apart the sentence. We recopy it on a sentence strip for the child to reread, but don't take time to cut it apart. At this point, most children can put the sentence back together easily and learn little from the activity. They have a good working knowledge of initial consonants and no longer have to puzzle through the task of putting the sentence in order. We don't want to do anything in the lesson that doesn't move the child along. So we drop it and save a minute or so for other parts of the lesson.

Introduction of a New Book

All aspects of this four-part lesson move forward in harmony. Now that Nick was well into the word family sorts, many of the books on levels 5 and 6 contained words with short vowels. When he came to word that he didn't know, I reminded him about patterns he could use in figuring out unknown words. The book reading, word study, and sentence writing flow together.

The book introduction follows the routines already described. I only did what I had to do for him to succeed in taking over the reading. Usually, we echo read the first several pages before Nick took over. Some days, when he needed extra support or the book seemed a bit long, I would read a page and then he would read a page. Then, if we had time, we would go back and read the page again, alternating reading, but this time reading pages that we had not read the first time.

Nick progressed steadily during these dark, winter months. He became more confident. He worked hard on his reading both during school and at home. Even with this steady growth, he still lagged behind most children in his class. His teacher and I agreed that he should remain in Early Steps for the rest of first grade. He was not ready for mid-year graduation.

Mid-year Graduation

By February about one-third of the children who began the program in the fall graduated from Early Steps. They were reading well in their first grade classroom.

After consulting with their classroom teachers and doing some informal assessments, we decided that these children would succeed without needing the intense instruction of Early Steps. They were reading level 8, 9 and 10 books fluently and had successfully completed the short vowel and long vowel (CVCE words) patterns. The tutor and classroom teacher agreed that they were reading well within the average range for first graders in their classroom. On the *End-of-the-Year Assessment*, described in chapter five, they read at least on the primer level.

February is the latest possible time to exit a child and pick up another to fill the child's slot. Most children need at least one semester of assistance to make significant progress. Therefore, we didn't add any new children to the program after the February graduation date. We replaced the graduates with first graders not originally identified for the program in the fall. Some of these children entered school during the year or just happened to make slower progress in reading than expected. The remaining two thirds of the children not graduating from the program participated in Early Steps for their entire first grade year.

Closing Comments

I looked forward to continuing my work with Nick for the rest of the year. Not only was Nick progressing well, but we had built a close relationship. Working day after day in a one-to-one situation gives both teacher and child an opportunity to grow together as close friends.

I often talked with our school counselors and my psychologist husband about the therapeutic relationships in Early Steps. The program builds upon a child's self-confidence. Each day the child leaves the lesson with a sense of accomplishment. The child tells you about his life particularly during sentence writing. The program brings rich rewards far beyond the specifics of each lesson. When you think about it, nothing is more important in life than rich human relationships. In the end I am not sure who benefits more--the teacher or the child.

Word Groups

Word Families

grade 1

cat	man	cap	sack
cat	man	cap	sack
mat	can	lap	tack
sat	van	nap	rack
pat	ran	tap	back
rat	fan	map	pack
flat	pan	sap	black
hat	plan	clap	track
	tan	snap	snack

grade 1

hit	big	win	sick
hit	big	win	sick
sit	fig	tin	kick
fit	wig	pin	lick
pit	dig	kin	pick
kit	pig	fin	tick
bit	twig	thin	trick
		chin	brick
		spin	stick
		skin	thick

grade 1

hot	too	sock	look
hot	too	sock	look
pot	pop	rock	book
lot	cop	lock	took
not	hop	block	cook
got	mop	clock	hook
dot	stop	knock	shook
spot	drop	shook	
	chop		

grade 1

cut	bug	run	duck
cut	bug	run	duck
nut	hug	gun	luck
but	dug	fun	suck
hut	rug	sun	stuck
shut	jug	spun	truck
	slug	bun	tuck
	mug		buck
	plug		cluck

grade 1

pet	red	hen	tell
pet	red	hen	tell
net	led	pen	sell
set	bed	men	fell
met	fed	ten	well
wet	shed	then	bell
let	sled	when	shell
jet			

VOWEL PATTERNS - I

grade 1		grade 1		grade 2	
hid	ride	girl	right	find	by
lip	nice	dirt	night	mind	my
win	bike	bird	light	find	fly
big	five	sir	might	climb	cry
kick	mile	first	bright	kind	sky
hit	side	firm	high	blind	fry
pin	drive	shirt	fight	grind	shy
trip	mine	birth	flight	child	spy
swim	dime	third	tight	wild	try
fit	wise			mild	
chin	shine				
this	slide				
	life				

VOWEL PATTERNS - A

grade 1		grade 1		grade 1		grade 2	
jam	lake	park	rain	day		fall	saw
ran	race	car	mail	say		ball	law
dad	tape	hard	wait	may		tall	paw
hat	page	barn	pain	way		call	raw
cab	same	jar	tail	pay		wall	claw
map	make	card	chain	clay		hall	draw
cat	name	far	paint	stay		mall	jaw
flat	take	part	maid	play		small	straw
clap	gave	farm	sail	tray			draw
back	trade	harm	paid	stray			
trap	shake	dart	stain				
that	made	start					
	cake	shark					

SHORT VOWELS

grade 1

bad	pig	mom	bus	pet
bad	pig	mom	bus	pet
hat	win	hot	cup	bed
ran	hit	job	nut	let
map	lip	top	fun	red
mad	kid	hop	cut	web
back	his	fox	bug	tell
had	sick	doll	but	less
has	sick	chop	shut	then
that	ship	chop	truck	when
glad	swim	drop	must	sled

VOWEL PATTERNS - E

grade 1				*grade 2*	
ten	feet	herd	he	meat	head
red	deep	germ	we	team	lead
beg	meet	clerk	she	lead	dead
get	feel	nerve	me	mean	bread
bell	free	serve	be	peak	deaf
less	green	her		clean	breath
nest	seed			beat	spread
left	need			dream	sweat
pet	queen			beach	
step	jeep			leaf	
sled	bleed			wheat	

VOWEL PATTERNS - O

grade 1				*grade 2*							
dot	go	rope	for	boat	book	told	moon	boil	cow	low	loud
job	no	note	corn	road	good	cold	roof	coin	how	snow	south
pot	so	hole	fork	soap	foot	colt	pool	soil	town	row	sound
mom		nose	born	load	look	gold	boot	point	plow	grow	mouth
top		coke	fort	coal	stood	fold	tool	noise	brown	show	shout
drop		hope	horn	loaf	hook	sold	shoot	spoil	crown	blow	count
jog		bone	pork	soak	brook	hold	tooth	voice	tower	flow	
lock		code	torn	coach	wood	mold	broom	boy	owl		
stop		woke	toast					toy			
bomb		stone	float								
shock		spoke	cloak								

VOWEL PATTERNS - U

grade 1			*grade 2*	
mud	cute	hurt	blue	new
cup	rule	burn	true	grew
bus	use	curl	glue	few
fun	rude	fur	clue	chew
rug	tune	turn	Sue	srew
club	huge	purr		flew
sun	June	nurse		blew
bug	fuse	curve		stew

Word Sort Instruction and Sequence

INSTRUCTION SUMMARY:

1. Headers must be known words
2. No more than three columns
3. No more than four words in column
4. Place word first then read the column (initially), so that word pattern assists the child.
5. When child can sort on own with little assistance, reinforce with spelling and with playing concentration.
6. When child can recognize most words randomly presented, child is ready to move on.

INSTRUCTIONAL SEQUENCE:

Stage 1: LETTER AND PICTURE SORTS

1. Letter recognition
2. Picture sorting
3. Picture and letter sorting

Stage 2 :WORD FAMILIES

1. Short a families: *cat   man   cap*-- drop one and add *back* family
2. Short i families: *hit   big   win*--drop one and add *sick* family
3. Review *a* and *i* families together
4. Short o families: *hot   top   sock*--drop one and add *look* family

Review *a's, i's, o's.*

DECISION: If child is quite adept, you can skip the short *e* and *u* word families and go straight to the short vowel groups. If word families have been somewhat of a struggle, do the short *e* and *u* families. These will probably go quickly.

5. Short *e* families: *pet   red   hen*--drop one and add *tell* family
6. Short *u* families: *cut   bug   run* --drop one and add *duck* family

Stage 3: SHORT VOWELS

1. Short *a, o* and *i* short vowels; no longer in families: *bad   mom   pig*
2. Drop one short vowel pattern and add the *u's*: *bad   mom   bus*
3. Drop one short vowel pattern and add the *e's*: *bad   bus   pet*

Stage 4: VOWEL PATTERNS

1. *jam   lake   park*-- drop one and add *ay* pattern
2. *hid   ride   girl* --drop one and *ight* pattern
3. *dot   rope   for*
4. *mud   cute   hurt*
5. *ten   feet   herd*--drop one and add *he* family

The remaining long vowel patterns are introduced in grade two.

Chapter 5
Spring

By spring, teachers new to Early Steps begin to see how the pieces of this program merge together to bring the child along. We can envision an overall pattern to the child's work. Before moving on, let's take a moment for reflection about where we have been and where we are headed. The chart on the next page will help put our discussion into perspective.

Putting the Pieces Together

Fall. During the first month, two learning hallmarks were concept-of-word and consonants. Children read books on levels 1-3. Many lacked letter knowledge. They started word study by learning to name and write the letters of the alphabet. Others knew most of the letters and began working on initial consonants through picture/letter sorts. Sentence writing mirrored this early semi-phonetic stage of development as they began applying letter knowledge in writing words with initial and sometimes final consonants. The children applied initial consonant knowledge in putting together the cut-up sentence. In book reading, I coached Nick to use initial consonant knowledge in figuring out new words. A variety of teaching strategies helped Nick gain an understanding of concept-of-word. Fingering-pointing, putting together the cut-up sentence, going back to text and pointing to a single word for the child to read and starting the word bank all worked together to clinch the idea that single words actually make up our written and spoken language.

Winter. When moving into level 4 and 5 books and the word family sorts, Nick started the challenge of vowels and built a deeper understanding of how initial consonants work. The books contained more words on each page, were slightly less predictable, and the picture support was not as tightly bound to text as before. Just relying on the book patterns and initial consonants was no longer enough. The child must now look beyond the initial letter to other letters in the word to untangle new words. Short *a* and then short *i* vowels came into play through the word families. Sorting word families drove home initial consonants and quietly moved the child into vowels. Quietly, because the vowels were nested within consistent rhyming or family patterns. The child's initial work with vowels

BOOK LEVEL WORD SORT	GOALS OR MAJOR EMPHASIS	STRATEGIES DURING BOOK READING	STRATEGIES AFTER BOOK READING
BOOK LEVEL: 1-3 WORD SORTS Letter identification Picture and letter sorts Beginning A families	Finger-pointing Concept-of-word Using memory and pictures	Echo-reading Rereading to find specific word Call attention to picture Call attention to known beginnings	Teacher (T) points to individual words Student (S) rereads to get word T. calls attention to beginning letter/sound
BOOK LEVELS: 4-5 WORD SORTS: A and beginning I families	Using context, pictures, beginning sounds Building word bank	Somewhat less echo reading Some partner reading Encourage use of beginning consonants Encourage self-correction, use of context	T. points to words S. begins to get some words without using context S. begins to use some word patterns to figure out words
BOOK LEVEL: 6-8 WORD SORT: short vowels	Confirming with beginning and ending consonants Uses vowels and vowel patterns student knows Self-correction	Echo reading limited to beginning and hard parts (mostly) S. reads up to unknown word, confirms guess by checking initial and final consonant and some vowels T. praises self-corrections	T. points to words, and S figures out from word patterns, letter sounds including short vowels and context
BOOK LEVEL: 8-9 WORD SORT: short, long e pattern, r controlled vowels	Moving toward independence Knowing more words at sight Using letter sounds and word patterns to figure out unknown words Orchestrating various cues	Echo reading limited to beginning pages of a story Confirm with all sounds in a word Some partner reading with student taking a larger part Review tricky parts	Point to words figured out during reading and talks about strategies used to read them successfully Discuss story
BOOK LEVEL: 10-12 WORD SORT: long patterns continued	Transition to classroom reading series Independence, fluency Large sight vocabulary Flexible use of phonetic elements	Limited echo reading Use of basal series on alternate days Comprehension and prediction questions Longer books may be read over two days and reread only as needed.	Review tricky parts Discuss story

occurred in a protected environment. In sentence writing, I pressed for short vowel patterns that Nick had sorted. In reading text, I assisted him in applying his emerging vowel knowledge to figuring out new words containing elements similar to those studied in word sorts.

Spring. In this chapter we begin where we left off--spring. We find greater variability among children, with some progressing much further than others. About a third of the original students have done so well that they have graduated mid-year. By March and April a majority of those remaining are usually reading books on levels 6 and 7 and have advanced to short vowel sorts which stress short vowels no longer cradled within rhyming patterns. Others are still on levels 4 and 5 and working on word families, while some of the more advanced students have progressed to level 9 and 10 books and are well into word sorts involving long and short vowels.

How did Nick fit into spring? Nick and I spent more time reading. We began to move more rapidly through word sorts. The sentence writing became less and less important. Let's take a closer look at where we were.

The Lesson

Rereading Familiar Books

I pressed Nick to read and reread more difficult level 6 and 7 books. He became more tolerant of applying strategies to figure out words on his own. In fact, he seemed to enjoy puzzling out unknown words in his reading. This was a welcome change from his previous intolerance about not knowing a word immediately.

With this new willingness, I took extra care to make sure the books were right for him. Keeping him on the instructional edge became more challenging. If books were too hard, he became frustrated and would shut down. This would set us back. We would move back to easier books for him to regain some confidence, before trying again.

Part of the challenge is that books classified in these mid to upper levels (7-9) vary considerably within and between levels. Some are more predictable than others. The print varies on the page. Vocabulary in some books is more sophisticated than others. Book selection actually becomes a bit tricky.

One way to check appropriateness of a book is to do an assessment or a reading record. While we do reading records throughout the year, these informal assessments become more useful when children are reading more complex text. The timing is right to talk about them in a bit more detail.

Reading Records

Reading Records play an important role when making decisions about when to move the child to the next level. Many of us remember these assessments as Informal Reading Inventories (Johns, 1997; Johnson & Kress, 1987) or more recently as Running Records (Clay, 1985). For those of you familiar with the work of Marie Clay, Reading Records are practically identical to Running Records used as part of the daily plan of Reading Recovery (Clay, 1985). However, these informal assessments play a less central role in Early Steps. While Reading Recovery teachers administer them daily to their students, we use them less frequently, perhaps two times per month for determining whether or not a book is appropriate and for gathering diagnostic information on the child.

Reading Records are brief assessments where the child reads a book read once (the previous day), but now reads again without any help from you. As the child reads, the tutor records any word recognition errors and then uses this information for making decisions about whether the book is working. Is it too easy, too difficult, or on a level where the reader can profit from instruction? The assessments also provide important information about word recognition strategies. For example, if she mispronounces two words beginning with *ch*, she probably needs extra help with this element.

Preparation. To prepare for the assessment, start at the beginning of the book and count out about 100 words. If the book contains fewer than 100 words, use the whole book. I find it easiest to photocopy the book so that I can write directly on my copy. However, this is not necessary. You and the child can use the same text. Record errors on another sheet of paper.

Administration. Hand the child the book and say, "Today, you get to read this book all by yourself. If you can't figure out a word, I will help you, but try."

Coding miscues. As the child reads, code reading behaviors. Don't intervene. Observe the child as you record miscues. When the child is stumped on a word, simply give the word after a brief wait time and make a note of it on your recording sheet. On your recording sheet, score miscues as *tolds*, *omissions* and *insertions*. Note self-corrections, but don't count as errors.

Scoring. After the child has completed the reading, score and analyze the miscues. For determining the accuracy score, count the number of words read. Then subtract the number of miscues the child made. Divide the number by the total number of words read and multiply by 100.

You can tell whether the text for the child is easy, instructional or too hard by using the following criteria:

Below 90% = hard
90%-94% = instructional
95%-100% = easy

For example, I wanted a more objective look at how well Nick was doing with level 7 books. I used the book, *All by Myself*, by Mercer Mayer. Notice his performance on the next page.

Interpretation. Nick made eight miscues and had two self-corrections on the selection. The book was at the upper end of his instructional level. It was challenging enough for him to get something out of it, but not too hard. When examining his word recognition errors, I saw that he had made good use of consonant blends in trying to figure out unknown words. Notice that he said *grass* for *ground* and *tram* for *trim*. At least he is getting the first part of the words correctly. Also, most of his

Level 7

All by Myself

I can get out of bed all by myself.

I can button my overalls. *ober-at* (SC)

I can brush my fur. *hair*

I can put on my socks and tie my shoes.

I can pour some juice for my little sister and help her eat breakfast. (T) (T)

I can pull a duck for her.

I can drive my truck.

I can ride my bike.

I can give a drink to my bear.

I can kick my ball and roll on the ground. *grass*

I can pound with my hammer. (T)

I can sail my boat. *send*

I can look after my little sister.

I can help Dad trim a bush or ice a cake for Mom. *tram* (SC) *fix*

I can look at a book and find a mouse.

I can color a picture. (T)

I can put my toys away and get into my pajamas.

I can brush my teeth.

I can put myself to bed but I can't go to sleep without a story. Good night.

$$\begin{array}{r} 130 \\ -8 \\ \hline 122 \end{array}$$

$$\frac{122}{130} \times 100 = 94\%$$

Total Words: 130	Instructional Level:
Errors: *8*	Hard
Accuracy *94*	Instructional *X*
Self-corrections *2*	Easy

85

substitution errors made sense-- *hair* for *fur*, *fix* for *ice*, *send* for *sail*. They weren't wild guesses. They fit the story context which indicates that he was comprehending the selection. He also succeeded in correcting two errors--this was a good sign.

Benchmark books. Teachers find it quite helpful to designate one or two books per level as benchmarks. These titles selected as representative for the particular levels are used most frequently for taking Reading Records.

We made benchmark selections rather unscientifically. Five teachers, all experienced with Early Steps and currently teaching one or more children, met together and independently decided the books at each level which seemed to be most representative. The teachers worked alone coming up with their own list first and then we worked together and came to a consensus about which books to designate as benchmarks. During the year, we tried them out with our students and then at the end of the year, met again and revised our list.

I use Reading Records for on-going assessment as well as for assisting with decisions about when to move the child to the next level. If the child does well with the Reading Record on the benchmark book, I feel more confident about shifting the child to the next level. Or, if the child struggles with it, the books on this particular level might be too hard. In this case, I find an easier book or go back a level for a while and consolidate knowledge before moving the child to more difficult books.

I reccomend setting aside benchmark books to use for Reading Records. When wanting more information on a child, introduce the benchmark book as a new book. The next day during rereading, use it for a Reading Record. Then take time to analyze the results. Use the data for making some inferences about the child's word study and book level needs.

Word Study

By the time we reach level 6 books, most children have progressed through the short vowel families. The child begins to hear differences in short vowels with the support of rhyming patterns and experiments with them in his writing. The next step is to clinch short vowel knowledge. We do this next through the short vowel sorts.

By late March, Nick had completed all of the remaining

word families. After the *i* families, we started the *o*'s. Then, we went back and reviewed the *i*'s and *o*'s together. Next, we moved to the *e*'s and finally the *u*'s. (See the word sort and instruction chart at the end of Chapter 4). In April Nick began the more advanced task of short vowel patterns. Before progressing, however, I did a simple assessment of his word family knowledge. Could he read words from the *a, i, o* and *u* patterns in random order (*bat, ran, hot, sit, plan, cut, fit, win*)? I put words from these categories in one pile and asked him to read them one-by-one. After doing this quite fluently, I knew he was ready for the short vowel patterns.

Short vowel patterns. Vowel patterns can be challenging. In the short vowel patterns, only the vowel sound and the spelling pattern (consonant-vowel-consonant) remain constant. The beginning and ending letters differ.

I began with three short vowels *a, i* and *o*, and used words that Nick already knew from the word families. I laid three known words on the table and said, "The words in this pile can be sorted under *can, pig* or *top*. We are trying to find words that have the same vowel sound." I took the word *cat*, pronounced it, and placed it under the *can* column. Nick did the next one. Each time a word was sorted, he read the words in the column.

can	pig	top
cat	sit	lot
lap	pin	job
bag	lip	stop

Word Sorting vs. Traditional Phonics. An important thing to remember is that word sorting is not a traditional phonics lesson. It is easy to misunderstand the word sort and ask the child to sound out an unfamiliar word before placing it in the column. The child pronounces each letter separately and then blends it together before placing it in the column. Think about what is happening here. This task is so abstract! The child processes the word as a single entity without support of other known words having similar features. This task is far more difficult for the child than first placing the known word in the correct column and then using the other words as support. Single letter sounding does not teach the child efficient word strategies.

Our language is made up of higher order patterns, and we must assist the child in using these patterns. Readers begin to see how the patterns in our language work and how to apply them to unknown words.   Mature readers recognize words through matching the unknown word with familiar patterns. This is far more efficient than matching sounds to single letters.

Don't talk about vowel sounds before children have made their own discoveries. Imposing knowledge from the outside doesn't take unless the child has already constructed the knowledge from within. Once children can do the vowel sorts fairly adeptly, we can then do quick mini lessons about short vowels. This is the time to make what you have done more explicit. "All of the words in this column have the same short *a* vowel sound. What is the short *a* sound that you hear in the middle as I say each of these words slowly--*can, cat, lap, bag*? Yes, the sound is /*a*/." Brief comments like these make sense after children have first discovered the concept for themselves. All we are doing now is giving them a label for what they have already learned. Talking about short sounds in the abstract wastes everyone's time. It is only after the child already gets it, that we teach the label. And, we don't make a big deal about it. Just mention it and move on. Always keep in mind that vowel labeling does not teach a child how to read.

Reinforcement Activities. As we progressed through the short vowel patterns, I reinforced Nick's knowledge with spelling, games and with reading the words in random order. Another reinforcement activity is Bingo.

I made two Bingo cards, one for Nick and one for me. Then, I selected three vowel patterns that we were reviewing and placed three header words for the patterns on both cards. I also put the headers in the same sequence for each card. For example, if we were reviewing the short *u, i* and *a* vowels, the headers on my card might be *cup, win* and *pat* and would be different words but follow the same sequence on Nick's card: *fun, lip* and *man*. Having our cards organized similarly, made the game somewhat easier and helped with the reinforcement of patterns.

Before we played, I made sure that we had at least eight words including the headers representing each of the patterns. I also tucked into the deck several free cards which work in any space on the Bingo card. After shuffling the cards, Nick rolled a dice to determine who went first. The first person to draw would look at the card, place it under the correct header and then read the header and the card. If either of us forgot to read the header and the word, we lost our turn. We continued to take turns until our Bingo cards were completely filled. In other words, we

cup	win	pat
bus	trip	fan
mud		flat
		Free ☺

fun	lip	man
drum	big	mat
	grin	plan
		sack

played blackout. If we were lucky enough to draw a free card, we could put it into any spot. The first one with a blackout was the winner.

A child must be solid with short vowels before progressing further. There is always a temptation to push too quickly, particularly with children who need more time to develop automatized knowledge. Be patient! By April Nick had worked through all of the five short vowel patterns. He could automatically read short vowel words such as *bug, ran, pat, hit, sock* randomly and could spell them confidently. The next step was the *a, a-e,* and *ar* patterns.

Vowel Patterns. Notice again, how we constantly add the new to the old. By comparing the known short vowels to the *a-e* and *ar* patterns, the child not only clinches old knowledge, but uses it for gathering in the new. By comparing the *cvce* words to the known *cvc* patterns, the child comes to discover the silent *e* generalization--the only generalization consistent enough in the English language to be worth teaching.

A similar understanding evolves with the *ar* words. By comparing the *ar* words with the known short vowel patterns, he gradually understands how the *r* changes the sound of the *a*. Once the child can sort, read, and spell them, you can have conversations about the final *e* generalization and how the bossy *r* works to control the vowel sounds. "What does the *ar* say in all of these words? What does that bossy *r* do to the *a* sound?"

The first sort looks similar to the following:

dad	lake	car
map	same	hard
back	take	far
hat	gave	barn

The procedure for instruction and reinforcement is identical to that already described. Let's review:

- The child must know the three header words.
- The first time through, the tutor and child take turns unless the child can immediately take over. The tutor supports only as needed.
- After placing the word in the column, the child reads the column.
- The following day or days after the child is becoming more automatic with a sort, reinforcement occurs through spelling, concentration, and bingo
- The child can move to the next word sort once he can read a randomized presentation of the words.

Once the child succeeds with the last step, he can move onto the *i's, u's* and *e's* (see Word Sort Chart, Chapter 4). With first graders we do not usually progress to the more complex vowel patterns such as the *ea* in *meat*, the *ai* in *rain*, the *oa* in *boat*, etc. These more complex patterns belong in second grade--even for the average to above average reader. Once children know the short vowels, the silent *e* generalization, and *r* controlled vowels, they have acquired a tremendous foundation. They have learned enough for grade one!

Sentence Writing

By late May, Nick wrote: *He is the frst tehr that is a gie* (He is the first teacher that is a guy.) Given that he had just started short *i, ir,* and long *i-e* group, I seized upon the opportunity to extend his emerging *ir* knowledge to his writing. We started with *first*. All I had to do was to pull out the *ir* words we had just sorted for him to change the spelling. Next, was the *ch* in teacher. "Nick, let's see if you can figure out what is missing in the word *teacher*. I think you can figure it out. It takes more than one letter to make the /*ch*/ sound." I made him sound boxes. He got it. I wasn't surprised. He already knew a lot about *ch* from previous word sorts.

Notice that I did not bother *teaching* about the *ea* in teacher and merely accepted the *e*. He wouldn't get any formal teaching on the *ea* element until grade two. Teaching about it would be wasted effort. But, look at his spelling of *guy* as *gie*. What a clever, informative mistake--a perfect example of testing out the final *e* generalization that he was in the midst of exploring through word sorts. Besides that his rendition made far more sense than the conventional spelling of *guy*. I decided not to go for the *er* in teacher. We had done enough. His revised sentence was:

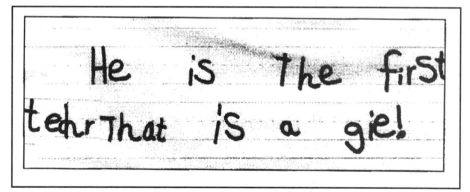

The *gie* in this sentence and the *plade* in another example below (*I played cliff hanger at my cousin's house*) are perfect instances of overextending. Watch for them. These smart errors indicate that the child is testing out hypotheses about our language. In both situations, Nick was working with the final *e* generalization. Even though he had previously written the word *played* correctly in earlier sentences, he now

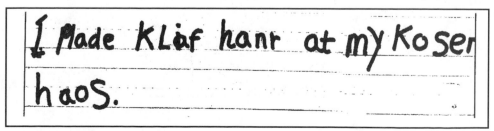

91

writes it with a final *e*. Now that Nick knew something about the final *e* generalization, why not try it out lots of times! As the child gains more control with an element, over-extensions start to disappear. We also talked about it. "Nick, you are really getting the idea about what that final *e* does to that vowel. I loved the way you wrote played. You can spell it another way? Do you remember how to spell it?" He fixed it.

Before leaving sentence writing, let's look at one last example. In early May Nick wrote --*I went to New Jersey*

What should I teach in this example? He has made three errors. What could he get with a little coaching? It made no sense to work with the *ew* in *new*. I decided to go after *went* and *Jersey*. Given that Nick had progressed well into the late stage of phonetic spelling, I decided to go for the *n* in *went*. As noted in our previous discussion about developmental spelling (Chapter 4), children in the phonetic stage of spelling development consistently omit *m* and *n* before the final consonant. These letters are difficult to hear because they collapse into the previous vowels. But now, he seemed ready for it.

I used sound boxes. "Nick, say the word *went* slowly. Do you hear any letter before the *t*?" After saying the word several times, he was able to hear the *n*. Another sign of progress!

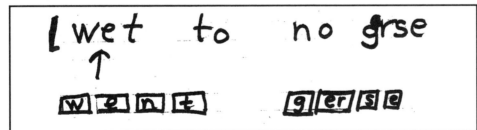

For the word, *Jersey*, I drew two boxes for the first syllable. I made the second box a little bigger so that he knew two letters could fit. Remember to put letters representing single phonemes--even those *r* controlled vowels into one box. One sound=one box. It worked. He wrote--

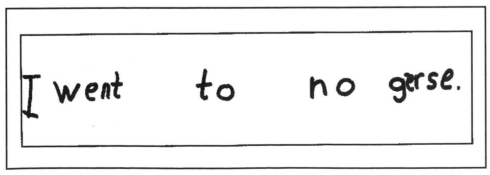

Dropping sentence writing. As children become more proficient readers, you will find that they get less out of the sentence writing. They become so good with phonetic spelling, that you find little to fix. This typically happens when the child begins reading about 8 and 9 level books. With Nick there were days toward the end of the year when there was nothing for me to teach in his sentence writing. Sometimes he spelled every word correctly. On these days, I did not rewrite his sentence on a sentence strip. He already had it right, so it made no sense for me to redo it.

By the end of the year, I dropped the sentence writing altogether. We began writing sentences two or three times per week. This gradual decline might surprise you. You are probably thinking--But isn't writing critical to the child's development? Yes, of course! The question is one of time. We have a half an hour and we need to spend it where the effort pays off the most. On the days when we didn't write, Nick spent more time reading. He was getting more out of this than writing. Besides that, he was writing a lot in Marilyn's classroom. So it made sense to begin changing the emphasis of our lessons.

Book Introduction

Level 8 books can be a bit intimidating. They are long with lots of print on the page. Nick sometimes balked when starting a hard book. So I did some bargaining. Sometimes we traded-off reading every other page. Nick would read a page, and I would read a page. When rereading the next day, he might read the whole thing, or we would trade off again, and I would read the pages he had read the previous day and vice versa. Another strategy with longer books was to use a book as the new book for two days. We would read the first half one day and the second half the next day.

As books increased in length, we also read fewer total books each day. For instance, we might only read two books at the beginning of the lesson and one at the end. Yet, we didn't decrease our total time reading. I always made sure that for at least half of the thirty minutes, we were reading books. The number of books read is not as important as the total number of minutes spent reading.

End of Year Assessment

During the last two weeks of school, we administer an *End of Year Assessment* to all of the children who participated in the Early Steps Program. We include children who had exited the program midyear as well as those added to the program during the year.

For this assessment, we must again thank Darrell Morris, who developed it in collaboration with his colleagues at Appalachian State University. We appreciate his permission to include it in this book. You will find it in Appendix D.

Notice that the assessment materials are organized into two parts. The first part contains information for the examiner. It includes ordering information for books, a list of materials, detailed directions for test administration, and the examiner's copy of the test. Part two includes the test packet which needs to be photocopied for each child being assessed.

The assessment includes three parts: Spelling, Word Recognition, and Book Reading:

Part 1: Spelling

The spelling test consists of 15 words. The first 12 are identical to those in the *ERSI*. There are three additional words added. Find the scoring sheet for spelling in the examiner's materials. The criteria for the spelling test are extended to include more advanced spelling features than were presented in the *ERSI*. Even with these changes you score it in the same manner as the *ERSI*. Award one point for each phoneme presented appropriately.

Name NICK

bacK baK back	5	dras	3
fet	3	pekt	3
Stape	3	Lap	3
R YJcK	2	rod	3
pikeing	5	pLant	5
maL	3	Short	5
Sid	3	grabeb	3
ij Jin	3		

It is always fascinating for the child to compare performance on the pre-test with that of the post-test. For Nick the results were dramatic. He didn't get any points for spelling on the *ERSI*. Even though he performed on low average when compared with the other children in the program, he did have a lot to be proud of. He had definitely made gigantic strides.

Part 2: Word Recognition

For the word recognition task, the child reads a list of 40 words frequently found in first and second grade reading materials. One point is awarded for each word read correctly. If the child is unable to read a word after about five seconds, move to the next one. Stop administering the test when the child makes seven consecutive errors. The score represents the total number of words read correctly. Nick received a score of 24.

Part 3: Book Reading

In this test the children read up to six passages progressing in difficulty as shown in the table below:

Level	Title
Emergent	*The Storm*
Pre-primer	*Look for Me*
Primer	*Mouse Tales*
1-2	*Frog and Toad All Year*
2-1	*Daniel's Duck*
2-2	*Wild, Wild Wolves*

The books were leveled previously by Darrell Morris and teachers participating in the Early Steps program. Such factors as predictability, the amount of print on each page, picture support, and vocabulary were all taken into consideration for determining levels. The book level equivalencies (emergent, primer, etc) represent an approximation of reading levels.

The children read 100 word passages from the book. They begin with the easiest selection and then progress as far as they can until meeting frustration level criteria. The criteria for stopping is 10% errors in word recognition and/or a reading rate of less than 40 words per minute. Reading slower than 40 words per minute can't really be classified as reading adequately.

Nick did well with passage reading through primer level. He fell below criteria on the l-2 selection. His word recognition performance was 85%.

As indicated from his test performance, Nick was not ready to exit the Early Steps program by the end of grade one. These results helped us make the decision to keep him in the regular Early Steps program for part of grade two. He continued in the program for the first three months of second grade before his classroom teacher and I felt he was a strong enough reader to succeed with the support of the second grade Early steps program where he met three times per week with a volunteer supervised by a trained Early Steps teacher.

Selecting Students. About 1/3 of the children who begin in grade one continue to need additional help in grade two. We can loosely classify second graders into two categories. One category of children will need more intense help. Falling within this group are children like Nick reading at the end of grade one on the primer level who will need support for several months, and those, who will need to participate in the program far longer. We always have a few children who take two years to progress to level 10-11 books. And for some children traditionally served in resource classrooms, the pacing is even slower. For example, several Downs Syndrome children continued in the first grade program for three years. Even though pacing is slower, they learned to read.

The other category of children includes those who are reading reasonably well, but are still behind their peers. They do not need a daily tutorial, but they still need help. The best option is for them to participate in the second grade Early Steps program where they receive one-to-one tutoring three times per week for about 40 minutes.

Program Organization. For the second grade program, a trained Early Steps teacher supervises the teaching of up to about six children at a time. The children are taught by parent volunteers, college students or retirees, but the Early Steps teacher plans each child's lesson. During the tutoring sessions, the volunteers do the actual teaching. All six children and the six volunteers are in the same room which allows the trained teacher to observe and make adjustments to the lessons. The teacher makes decisions about what each child reads and his or her needs for word study. The teacher has the books and the word sorts ready when the volunteers arrive so that all they have to do is teach the lesson.

We start the second grade program with about a three hour inservice for volunteers where we explain the program and model demonstration lessons. For the first week, the volunteers just read with the children, which assists everyone in becoming comfortable with the situation. By the second week they begin teaching the program.

Program components. The second grade lesson has three parts. The children spend the first fifteen minutes reading (part one). Often, they read selected stories from old basal readers that support the child with more controlled vocabulary and prescribed book levels. Following the reading is word sorting (part two). By second grade word sorting is more sophisticated focusing on short and long vowel patterns, as well as the more complex patterns (*oi, aw*, etc). See the word sort chart for a listing of second grade patterns (Chapter 4). Part three is book reading. Often these books are small chapter books which may last several days.

Each child has a notebook with a daily log where the Early Steps teacher has listed the books and the word sorts the child is to do for the lesson. When the volunteers arrive, they take the child's notebook, review the plans and begin tutoring. While the volunteer and the child are working, the Early Steps teacher monitors each child's performance. Immediately after the lesson, the Early Steps teacher plans the next lesson for each child.

Closing Comments

The second grade component is critical to the success of children needing a slower pace of instruction. Our research definitely shows that Early Steps is working to improve the achievement of children most in danger of failing in reading (Santa & Høien, in press). But, no reading program guarantees success *for all* readers.

We are not going to fix everyone in first grade. Many continue to need further help. We must insure that this happens! I have seen many children who progress slowly in grade one but who then surge ahead in grade two. Some simply take longer to gain a solid foundation for later success. Our precious human investments need continual monitoring and nourishment.

Chapter 6
Early Steps in the Classroom

By: Carol Santa and Roxanne Gallup

Early Steps does not stop with individual tutoring. It spills naturally into classroom instruction, particularly for teachers who have tutored individual children in the program. Teachers find many applications to both small and large group instruction.

I feel fortunate to collaborate in writing this chapter with a REAL first grade teacher, Roxanne Gallup. Roxanne, who teaches in a small public school in my community, started her involvement in Early Steps during our first year of implementation. She tutored one of her first graders and participated in the graduate class led by myself and Darrell Morris. In this chapter we describe how she integrates Early Steps into her language arts curriculum so that every first grader in her class benefits.

Teacher knowledge

Successful classroom implementation begins with teacher knowledge. The only clear way to gain this knowledge is through tutoring an individual child within a supervised collaborative environment. Roxanne and I can't stress this enough. Classroom teachers must individually tutor at least one child before they can successfully infuse elements of the program into the larger context of their classroom. Our reasoning is simple. You must learn how the process works first individually before understanding the program's potential for implementation with the more complex classroom situation.

In fact, we recommend, even after the first year, that classroom teachers continue to do some tutoring. Each tutoring situation presents a unique and rewarding laboratory for our own learning. Treat yourself to learning from a child. We owe it to ourselves to continue improving our own skills as learners.

Creating time

With some creative scheduling most teachers can carve time from busy schedules to tutor. Some tutor during the time taken by special classes taught by librarians, art, music and physical education teachers. Others organize their daily schedules for parent volunteers and Title One tutors to take over their classrooms for a half hour per day leaving them time to tutor. While the teacher works with a child, the rest of the class listens to stories read aloud or works in small guided reading groups led by volunteers or Title One tutors. These situations are ideal both for the teacher and the child because tutoring comes out of the regular classroom day.

Some teachers end up tutoring during their planning period or before or after school. For example, Roxanne's school has insufficient support staff. Her district is too small for special art, music, and physical education teachers, and she has had difficulty finding dedicated volunteers. Therefore, she tutors one child before school. She tried tutoring after school, but both she and her child felt too exhausted to concentrate very well. Early Steps lessons demand energy from both the child and the teacher. Timing is critical. The extra effort for tutoring creates some hardships, but teachers still find it invaluable for the child and for themselves.

Now that we have expressed our strong convictions about classroom teachers continuing to tutor, we move to the actual topic of this chapter which is about classroom implementation. We begin this discussion with ways to use the *Early Screening Reading Instrument (ERSI)* as a tool for gathering information on students and for instructional planning. Then, we discuss how to implement many elements from Early Steps into small group instruction.

The Early Reading Screening Instrument (ERSI)

Roxanne administers the *ERSI* to each child in her class. About the third week of school she begins the assessments with assistance from parent volunteers and Title One tutors. Even though it takes about 20 minutes per child, the time is well worth it. She gathers a wealth of information.

Student knowledge. The assessment provides an individual portrait of each child's literacy knowledge. For example, Roxanne gains insight into every child's alphabet knowledge which she uses for planning individual and small group instruction specifically to meet needs. She also identifies children who don't yet have an understanding of concept-of-word. She knows which children to observe and monitor to insure the development of this critical understanding.

The spelling assessment provides information about individual development of phonemic awareness. She learns about each child's phonemic knowledge and where to begin teaching. Most children, who know their letters and can represent most initial and final consonants in their spelling, are ready for word family sorts. Others scoring at the lower end of the scale in both letter and phonemic knowledge will need to begin with picture sorts and alphabet practice.

The assessment also identifies children already reading some sight words. For these children Roxanne will do some additional informal assessments to identify their instructional levels, so that she can provide them with appropriately challenging materials.

Instructional decisions. In addition to learning about each child, Roxanne uses the information to make both management and instructional decisions. She can look at the results and answer some questions: What concepts should I teach to the whole class? What is most appropriately taught in small groups or individually? For example, not everyone needs work with the alphabet. Do I need to review this with the whole class or should I just teach it to the individuals who need it? Which children are already reading? As Roxanne comes up with answers to these questions, she starts to structure her classroom to meet the individual strengths and needs of her students.

Forming small groups

Roxanne uses data gathered from the *ERSI* to make preliminary grouping and instructional decisions. The children falling toward the end of the distribution, the lowest three to five students, will receive Early Steps tutoring as well as participate in a small group focusing on their specific skill needs. As part of their small group instruction, she will include work with learning letters and initial consonant sounds as well as experiences in reading together predictable big book stories and in developing language experience stories.

The five to six children in the middle range will form a second group. With these children she will spend several weeks reviewing initial letter sounds while simultaneously introducing them to easy level one reading selections. The children in the upper third of the distribution form her most advanced group. Some are already reading, and the rest are ready to begin formal instruction. She will begin with word families and start the group with level two and three books.

Clustering children from information gathered from the *ERSI* provides a good place to begin. None of her groups remain static. The division between groups in some instances varies by only a few points which makes these divisions quite arbitrary and necessarily fluid. Children within groups progress as soon as groups are formed. Roxanne constantly shifts students among groups so that each child is kept on the instructional edge.

Descriptive stages for group participation

As children progress through the year, Roxanne finds it helpful to think about groups at various stages in their reading development. Students progress differently, but they move through a similar developmental progression. She organizes students into small groups based on a four-stage descriptive continuum: *Experimenting Readers, Emergent Readers, Capable Readers* and *Independent Readers*. Her more advanced students, those in the top quartile of the *ERSI*, move more rapidly through this continuum than readers performing in the mid and lower quartiles of the *ERSI*. Some children struggling with reading may progress only as far as the emergent level by the end of the year. These children, even those supported by Early Steps, will likely need reading support into grades two and three.

Having a conceptual framework for defining groups and for monitoring student progress helps Roxanne plan for instruction. She uses the following reader and book criteria to describe each stage and to organize her groups:

Experimenting Readers

Reader Characteristics:
- may not demonstrate concept-of-word
- still learning letter/sounds
- sorting picture cards
- writing using some initial letters

- growing sight vocabulary--up to about 30-50 words

Book characteristics:
- simple story structure
- pictures tell the story
- repetition with only one or two word changes on each page
- rhyming
- Early Steps levels: 1-4

Emergent readers

Reader characteristics:
- grasps the basics of print
- uses more than one cue (context, initial consonant, word family patterns) to self-correct
- sorts word families
- writes with initial and final consonants, some vowels, and finger spaces
- sight vocabulary: 80-130 words

Book Characteristics:
- more complex story structure
- longer sentences
- pictures not as connected to the story
- sentence structure becomes more complex
- increased text on each page
- Early Steps levels 4-6

Capable Readers

Group characteristics:
- self-corrects with little teacher intervention
- sorts short vowels or vowel patterns
- uses short vowel patterns in writing
- understands concepts of story: problem, character, and setting
- sight word vocabulary of 130-270 words

Book characteristics:
- more complex story structure
- fewer pictures and more text per page
- Early Steps levels 6-8

Independent Readers

Group Characteristics
- self-corrects with little/no teacher intervention
- sorts vowel patterns
- consistently uses vowel patterns in writing
- extensive sight vocabulary

Book characteristics:
- more complex story structure
- few pictures and more text per page
- longer books and easy-to-read chapter books
- Early Steps levels 8+

Continual monitoring of performance. The book characteristics appropriate for each stage are critical to the child's development. Books can neither be too hard nor too easy. They must be challenging enough for children to learn something, but not too difficult.

Roxanne monitors and evaluates the children through observation and reading records (see previous chapter) to insure that books match instructional needs. The reading should provide the children with a small amount of new learning. If the text is too easy, children have little chance for reading development and with texts that are too difficult, children don't even have an opportunity to read.

She strives to select books within the children's instructional range so they are reading with more than 90% accuracy. It is at this range that the child can benefit most from instruction. Reading records let her know immediately when the reading process becomes a struggle. When accuracy rates begin to fall below 90%, the child starts to labor over sounding out words which reduces the possibility of reading for meaning.

A good rule-of-thumb is to do reading records on every child, particularly those in the lower group from once to twice a month. In this way, the teacher knows about the individual growth of the child and when to shift children among groups. Children learn so quickly that we need an ongoing record of their performance. The accuracy rate lets us know if we are selecting books at the appropriate level for our students and if a student is working in the most appropriate group.

Reading Materials

Leveling books. Roxanne worked with other primary teachers in her school to organize reading materials according to a continuum of difficulty. They gathered together a variety of older and newer basal pre-primers, basal anthologies, and multiple copies of books and organized them into progressive levels. They then used district funds to fill in the holes of the continuum with additional titles. They purchased from five to seven copies of the same title to use for small group lessons and have gradually added to their book collection over the years.

The teachers use the same procedure for leveling of books as described previously for Early Steps. Book leveling is not exact science. The ease or difficulty of a book is always an individual matter depending on the child's experiences and word knowledge. Even though this is the case, they use the following parameters for approximating book levels:

- The amount of text on the page
- Print size and spacing between the words
- Picture support of text
- Placement of text on page
- Text predictability
- Vocabulary
- Complexity of story line

Organizing materials. The teachers in Roxanne's school store their book collection in a central location. They organize titles sequentially by level of difficulty on library stack shelves and have developed a check-out system to keep track of titles. Given that books are only used for several days by one small reading circle, the books are easily shared among kindergarten, first and second grade teachers. They have gradually added to their collection through book clubs and classroom library purchases. By pooling all resources and housing them in one place, the collection quickly grows.

Managing small groups

Roxanne uses a reading rotation schedule as the basic management plan for small group instruction. She blocks her mornings into 30 minute time frames. At the beginning of the year, she uses twenty minute blocks when her students are not quite so independent.

Roxanne's students welcome the structure of the schedule and become familiar with what comes next. As shown in the chart below, students in each group rotate through each of these three blocks: reading circle, centers and independent activities. She keeps a copy of this chart posted in her classroom for student reference.

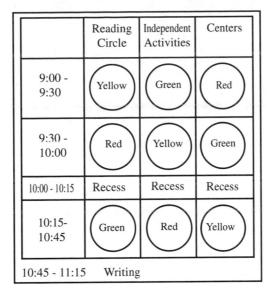

	Reading Circle	Independent Activities	Centers
9:00 - 9:30	Yellow	Green	Red
9:30 - 10:00	Red	Yellow	Green
10:00 - 10:15	Recess	Recess	Recess
10:15 - 10:45	Green	Red	Yellow
10:45 - 11:15	Writing		

Centers. To implement this schedule, she prepares center activities which might include painting easel, writing center, math manipulatives, science activities, computer time, and a listening center. The challenge is to have center activities that engage student interest and independent participation so that she can meet with each group.

Independent activities. The children spend another block of time doing independent activities. These include journal entries, independent reading assignments, sight word practice, and other activities assigned in the reading circle.

In addition to Roxanne's plan, teachers have found other ways to manage reading groups. In the best situation, they will have all of their small groups at the same time. Teachers invite special teachers into the classroom for a thirty minute reading period. They ask Resource teachers, Title One teachers, and any parent helpers into their room and have each take a group so that small group reading happens to everyone at the same time. The classroom teacher usually takes a different group each day as a way to keep track of children's performance. In most situations, the teacher also plans the lessons for each group. This would include the selection of reading materials and word study activities.

Small Group Instruction

Small group instruction contains the same features as an Early Steps lesson. From one-half to two-thirds of the time is spent in the reading and rereading of small books and stories. The remainder of the time is spent with word study activities.

The lesson changes to reflect the developmental stages of children in the group.

Reading and Rereading

Guided reading. Roxanne uses a variety of guided reading procedures to insure that all children in the group spend the majority of time in the lesson reading. (For an excellent resource on guided reading see Fountas & Pinnell, 1996.) With guided reading, everyone participates. It is not a round-robin traditional basal lesson where children take turns reading aloud. Instead, every child reads the entire selection. No one has to wait his turn. Students divide into pairs and read the selection together. The teacher guides the children to figure out unknown words, untangle sentence structure, and learn new concepts. The goal is for children to learn how to use reading strategies successfully and independently.

Rather than pre-teaching vocabulary before the lesson by listing the words on the board and talking about them, Roxanne begins by taking the children on a walk through the story. On this walk, she does an Early Steps book introduction by talking about the pictures and any potentially difficult words and concepts. She familiarizes the children to the point that they can either read or almost read the story on their own. Upon completing the walk, the children turn back to the beginning of the book and begin reading.

During the reading, the children use cues to gain information from text. She steps in when necessary to assist them in figuring out new words or ideas through strategy prompts. After reading, the children talk about the story, returning to the text to share ideas and to problem solve. This shared discussion is quite different than the post-reading activities prevalent in traditional basal lessons where the teacher asks the children lists of comprehension questions. It is far more collaborative and student directed. The guided reading lesson typically ends with the children rereading the story in pairs for practicing their reading fluency.

Her guided reading lessons differ according to the various stages of reading development. During the first few months, each group will need far more direction than later in the year when they begin to read more independently. Let's look more closely at two guided reading sequences, one for an early emergent group and another for a more advanced group.

Guided Reading: Early Emergent

1. Story Introduction and Picture Walk

- Talk about the title and make predictions about what the story will be about.
- Go through the story, page by page, reserving the last two or three pages, particularly if the story line contains a twist at the end.
- As you page through the story, talk about what is happening on each page using vocabulary on the pages. Point to some of words which children may not know as you talk.

2. First Reading

Provide enough support in the first reading for students to begin reading it on their own. Begin with the title. Read and finger-point it. Have the students do the same thing. Then begin reading and finger-pointing the first one or two pages until the predictability of the book allows the children to take over.

- Read aloud the first several pages.
- Point to the words as you read.
- After you read a page, ask the children to read it together (echo read).
- Remind them to read it with their finger.
- You read a page; the children read the page. Continue echo reading until the children begin to get the pattern and begin reading it on their own.
- Only support the children until they can take over. With some children in the group you will need to support them a bit more.

3. Second Reading

Most children will be able to read the story the second time by themselves. Support only as needed.

- The children read the story orally together. Let each read at their own pace.
- Observe and guide the children.
- After they read, go back to the beginning and go through several pages, pointing to a word. Ask, "What word is this?"
- Observe the strategies of each child. Does the child reread the sentence pointing to each word until coming to the word? Does the child know the word without rereading? Can the child finger-point the words correctly indicating concept-of-word?

4. Rereading

Just as in the Early Steps lessons, rereading is critical for building the children's confidence and for the initial acquisition of sight vocabulary. Children need many opportunities to know what fluent reading feels and sounds like.

- The children reread the book themselves or in pairs the next day.
- Over the next several days invite them to reread the story again on their own.

5. Strategy Knowledge

During the reading and rereading assist the children in using and becoming aware of strategies. Think about ways to turn strategy knowledge over to them so they can begin applying strategies on their own. Provide opportunities for children to reflect on what they know about applying strategies for solving their own reading challenges. At this early emergent level, prompt them to use strategies based on knowledge that they already know.

Letter/sound strategies:

- Look at the first letter. Use that first letter to help you.
- Does that word start with a...?
- What word has the right sounds to fit here?
- We have had this word before. Let's go back and find it on the page you just read.

Meaning Strategies:

- Let's read this line and skip the word. What makes sense?
- Look at the picture. What words go with the pictures?
- Does that sound right?
- Does that go with the story?
- Does that make sense?
- What other word would make sense here?

Strategy-use cues:

Once children have figured out the word, go back and reinforce a child's recognition of a word with prompts similar to these:

- How did you know this word is_____?
- What do you do when you come to a word you don't know?

6. After Reading

After reading and rereading a book, do one or two informal comprehension activities. With early emergent texts containing few words on each page, it is difficult to do much with comprehension instruction--there is little in level one and two books to comprehend. With longer texts, ask one or two questions or have the children briefly retell the story. Students can retell the story individually or in a round-robin fashion. Retelling is a valuable tool for practice in sequencing and for checking comprehension.

After completing a book, introduce the children to another book on about the same level of difficulty. So, within a 20 minute guided reading time, the group might read two or three books. With shorter, more patterned books, they may even read up to four books in one session. The first two or three books might be rereads--books read over the past several days--while the last one will be a new, perhaps slightly more challenging book. After introducing the book, children will read it at least once. This new book will then become one of the rereads for the next guided reading session.

Guided Reading: Capable Readers

As groups advance, the number of books read in one guided reading session will change. Given the increasing difficulty and length of the books, children will likely read only one or perhaps at most two books within a twenty to thirty minute session. The key factor is not the number of books read, but that children spend most of the session reading.

1. Story Introduction

Toward the end of grade one, when children have become more independent with reading, the story introduction changes. Provide just enough support for them to read the selection successfully.

- Ask students to help you figure out the title.
- Together page through the book and talk about vocabulary or language patterns that might be challenging.
- Ask students to predict story events.

2. First reading

Together develop several focus questions and then ask students to read and find answers to the questions. Model reading only as needed. This might mean reading aloud the first one or two pages before students read it on their own.

- Students read selection quietly.
- Support individual children as needed.
- Guide their reading with one or two focus questions.
- Ask students to read aloud information from text which supports or confirms answers to questions.
- Encourage students to discuss any print problems and solutions.
- Talk about strategies to use when coming to unfamiliar words or language patterns.

3. Second Reading

Ask students to read silently again. Guide and observe them as they read. Check comprehension through story retelling.

Some other alternatives:
- Pair children. Ask students to reread the book together to practice fluency. Pair students so that one child reads the even, the other the odd pages. Then switch odd/even roles and ask pairs to read the story again.
- Reread aloud as a reader's theater.

110

4. Strategy Knowledge

During every aspect of the lesson, remind children about using strategies for figuring out unknown words and for comprehending meaning. Use prompts to help them internalize a system of strategies which they can apply on their own to increasingly more complex text. Rather than simply giving children words or clarifying meaning, hold back. Why is it that we itch to give answers, to jump in, to take over? The more we do, the less children do on their own. How can our children become confident problem-solvers when not given the opportunity to solve their own problems? So, when a child gets stuck, sit on your hands and instead of quick answers, use prompts.

Focus on word prompts such as:

- Why did you stop reading?
- Look at the first letters.
- What word makes sense here?
- Leave the word out and read to the end of the sentence. What would fit?
- Do you know another word that looks like this word? (Remind students of a particular word sort.)
- Do you know a word that has the same pattern?
- Do you know a word that starts/ends with these same letters?
- You made a word mistake. Can you find it in this sentence?
- Try that again. What word sounds right?

Focus on meaning prompts such as:

- Does this make sense?
- What do you think will happen next?
- Does that sound right?
- Try again. What would make sense?
- How can you help yourself?
- You almost got it! What can you do now?

Focus on the child's use of self-correction strategies:

- I liked the way you figured that out.
- Can you find your mistake?
- I am not sure that sounded right. Read it again.
- You almost got this right. Try again.

Through prompting, students will begin considering these questions for themselves when applying strategies on their own. The challenge is balance. As the child gains more control, our support lessens. We move in and out as the children take over processing for themselves.

Radiant Readers

Another reading and rereading procedure similar to the guided reading strategies just described, is a sequence which we call Radiant Readers. For this sequence, we have borrowed ideas from the work of Jim Hoffman (Hoffman and Crone, 1984) and Darrell Morris (Morris and Nelson, 1992). These researchers have developed some effective strategies for small group reading which build reading achievement.

The Radiant Reader sequence occurs over a three day period:

Day 1. Listening and Echo reading

1. The teacher fluently and expressively reads the story aloud. The teacher stops several times during the reading to ask several clarification and prediction questions: Why do you think the character did this? What do you think is going to happen now?

2. The teacher then echo reads the story with the children. The teacher reads a page with the children following along. The children then go back and reread the page--mumble reading in unison.

Day 2. Partner reading

1.   The children divide into pairs--a stronger reader with a weaker one. The teacher assigns children to read every other page. For the first reading, one child reads the odd pages, the other the even.

2. Then the children switch from odd to even or even to odd and read the pages they had not previously read. The pairs assist one another.

3. The teacher moves from pair to pair listening and assisting the children.

4. The teacher assigns each child a page or several pages to read for radiant reading. The children practice their assignment until they read it radiantly.

Day 3. Radiant Readers

1. The children then take turns reading their assigned parts either to the group or to the teacher.

2. As the child reads either in the group or individually to the teacher, the teacher evaluates the child's reading doing a reading record.

3. After each child reads, the group discusses what the reader did to be so radiant. "You read so quickly." "You only missed one word." "You did so well in figuring out that word all by yourself." The children's names then go up on the radiant reader chart, or they get a sticker after their names.

While the Radiant or Expert sequence works well during the beginning of the year, it also assists children as they advance in their reading development. Later in the year you will need to do some modifications. For example, the first day will look quite different. You won't need to do as much modeling. But, assigning students to read odd or even pages for paired reading and practicing for radiant reading performances are important strategies for the entire year.

When children have these opportunities to practice for fluency, they begin to understand what it means to be an accomplished reader. These radiant performances also give you opportunities throughout the year for conducting some informal evaluations and for students to discuss radiant reader qualities.

Independent Reading

In addition to the reading that occurs in small groups, Roxanne has also developed a system to insure that students have daily opportunities for independent reading. She has organized her classroom library into a series of storage bins or plastic dishpans. The books in each bin are on approximately the same level of difficulty. In her classroom collection are old pre-primers, books from the Early Steps program, as well as others she has purchased from book clubs and checked out from the school library. She also includes any books previously introduced to the children in small groups as part of guided reading lessons or as radiant reader sequences.

Roxanne insures smooth management by coding each bin and the books in the bin with colored sticky dots. For example, she might put all of the easiest books into the bin identified with a yellow sticky dot. Each book in the bin also has the same yellow sticky dot on the front cover of the book. Books at a slightly higher level would be put together into the next bin coded with a blue sticky dot, etc. This bin and sticky dot system helps the children know where each book belongs. It also assists the teacher in directing children to a specific collection of books appropriate for their particular reading levels.

114

She gives each child a folder. On each folder Roxanne places a sticky dot indicating which collection the child is to use. Inside the folder she places a Reader's Log for children to record the books from the bin they read.

When children are reading the easiest books, which are normally about five pages long with minimal text on the pages, Roxanne challenges her students to read them multiple times for fluency. For example, the children might read a book three times to themselves, once to a classmate, and then to a teacher. The teacher might be a third or fourth grade reading buddy, a parent, a grandparent volunteer or Roxanne. Each time the children reread, they keep track by making a tally mark on the contract. The classroom buddy and teacher also initial the contract after the child reads the book to them. Roxanne informally monitors children's performances and moves children from one bin level to another.

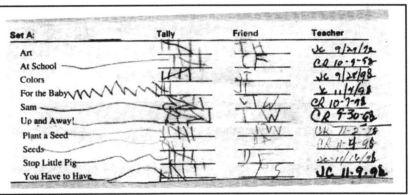

This management plan turns out to be an excellent way to introduce Reading Workshop into a first grade classroom. The students have extensive guidance on what to read, but still can make some choices. The procedure also insures that students progress systematically through a leveled sequence of books appropriate to their own instructional levels. Besides that, the children know exactly what they are supposed to do each day, which leaves Roxanne about 20 minutes per day to attend to some individual needs or meet with a small group.

Word Study

Roxanne finds that most elements of an Early Steps lesson can be implemented with little or no preparation. Word sorts are an exception. Preparing them does take planning and organization, but the time is well worth the effort. Including word sorts as part of small group lessons can become a complete phonics program or a powerful supplement to any existing program.

Organizing materials. Roxanne has parent volunteers assist her in preparing ten sets of the picture and word cards, which are then laminated, cut apart and organized into labeled file boxes. Even though this initially takes effort, she uses these same materials for several years.

She also cut up several large pocket charts into individual charts. Once cut apart, she reinforces the edges of the individual charts with plastic tape. Having individual charts available for word sorts helps children become more organized and saves time.

Introduction to sorting. The word sort introduced in a group depends upon the stage of reading development. For the most advanced students, Roxanne will start in the fall with

word families. With children scoring in the lowest quartile of the *ERSI*, she will begin with letter and picture sorts. Her procedure for initially introducing the children to sorting is similar for all groups.

Roxanne sits facing the group. Using a pocket chart, she places the guide words, pictures or letters in the chart and begins with modeling. As she demonstrates, she verbalizes her thinking:

Let's read these three words (pictures).
Maybe this one goes here-*cap, lap, mat*
No, it doesn't sound or look right.
I think it goes here.
Let's see...*hat, cat, mat...*
Yes! *Mat* belongs here.

The next few lessons require less teacher direction. Working with the same set of cards, she passes the word set out to the students. She sits facing the group with a pocket chart displaying the header words (letter, pictures) across the top. Each child individually comes up to the pocket chart and places his or her word in the correct column. Then everyone reads the column aloud. As a group, the children decide if the word is in the right place. If not, a child volunteers to change it and everyone reads the column again. The group sorts all of the words in this manner for several days until students become comfortable with the process.

Once students understand how to do the sorts, they begin sorting independently in the group. Roxanne passes out the individual pocket charts and a set of words clipped together. She has the three header words posted in the group pocket chart. Each child sorts, reciting each column aloud (quietly) as they add a word. Roxanne moves from one child to another listening to them each read their entire sort. After reading the sort, each student pulls all of the words from the pocket chart, clips them together and gives them to Roxanne to keep until the next day. As a variation, Roxanne might say each word out loud and have students find and pull that word from their pocket chart. Or, students may take turns selecting and saying words to remove and put away.

Reinforcement and assessment. Once a week Roxanne has each group do a spell check. The spell check serves to reinforce and assess knowledge of the sort featured during a particular week. Children divide a sheet of writing paper into three parts. They record the date at the top and then write the words as dictated. After completing the list, Roxanne passes out colored pencils for the children to check their own work. She wants her students to have immediate feedback about what to fix in their spelling.

Self-correcting their spelling work is in itself a mini lesson. Roxanne guides the children in saying each word aloud and breaking it into phonemes. As the children verbalize each sound, they say the letter/letters that stand for the sound.

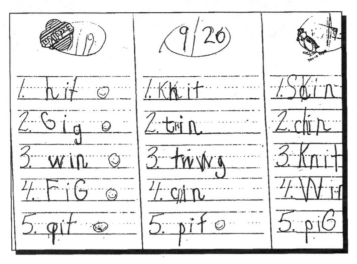

Teacher: Cat../k/ (the sound for *k/c*)
Students: It's a *c*.
Teacher: /*a*/
Students: It's an *a*
Teacher: /*t*/
Students: The letter *t*!

The spell check, when used front to back, provides a six week record of each student's development. It becomes a valuable tool for reporting to parents and providing data for making decisions about moving a child to a different group. Roxanne includes spell check records in each child's reading portfolio. The records also provide the teacher with a clear indication about when it is time to move a group to the next word sort sequence.

Changing sorts. Roxanne has a precise way to change word sorts in a group so that it doesn't become a management nightmare. She recommends not changing more than one group's sort at a time--at least not at first.

When it is time to move to the next sort, she has the group sort the words as they normally would. Then, she collects one word at a time from all of the students. She clips the words together as the children pass them to her for storage in a small

118

file box. She passes out the next words in the same way--one word at a time. Students then clip their word sets together. Roxanne always collects the individual sets from each child before dismissing the group. She puts the word sets into a file box ready to pass out to the children at the next circle meeting.

Sentence Writing

Roxanne does not usually do daily sentence writing in the small group. By the time students read and complete their word sorts, she has run out of time.

She reserves sentence writing for another part of the day. Her children write daily in their journals. On most occasions they write a sentence of their choice. Sometimes, however, she dictates a sentence which includes words children have met in word sorts or as part of their reading.

Roxanne incorporates the strategy of having children say the sentence before they write and then teaches them to say words aloud as they write and to listen to the sounds. She introduces this through whole class demonstrations. For example, in the beginning of the year, her modeling will go something like this:

"When we write, it will help if you say the words aloud. Who can help me write this sentence--*My cat is home*? Say the first word. What do you hear at the beginning of *my*? Say the word again. What letter do you hear on the end of the word *my*?"

Roxanne continues to model, saying and writing each word. At this point, she only writes letters the students give her. For example, she wouldn't bother pushing for the silent *e* in the word *home*. She knows that her children aren't ready for the final *e* generalization this early in the year. Her goal during this initial teaching is to help her students feel comfortable with writing phonetically.

Some teachers like Roxanne have each student keep a sentence book similar to that used in Early Steps tutoring. The children write one or two sentences a day. As students write, Roxanne moves quickly from child to child doing some individual teaching. Her goal is to meet with each child briefly, once per week during writing time. The children's sentence books or journals provide an important record of each child's development. When children fill up all of the pages in their writing books, Roxanne keeps them as part of the child's portfolio.

Concluding Comments

Over the last decade we have seen a renewed and welcome emphasis on helping children with reading difficulties. Teachers have made tremendous strides in helping children become readers through one-to-one programs such as Early Steps. Yet, the power of any intervention program is whether or not methodologies can be transferred from individual situations to the regular classroom. Our goal is to have coordinated instruction so that children receive similar teaching in tutorials and in the classroom. Children make the most rapid progress with cohesive instruction.

When an intervention remains in the hands of a few, a program makes little impact. Only a few teachers benefit; only a few children receive help. Yet, in our society every child deserves the best possible instruction. Early Steps must become deeply imbedded within a system. It can't remain exclusive, owned by a few experts in a school. Principals, classroom teachers, Title One Teachers, Resource teachers and volunteers can become Early Steps teachers with commitment and training. Deep implementation occurs when expertise is shared within a broad community of learners.

The knowledge gained from teaching and learning from individual children has enriched and changed our understanding of how children learn to read. Our involvement in Early Steps has created a research environment in our schools where teachers constantly revise their theories about how children learn. We catch ourselves observing, reflecting, and talking shop far more than before.

Roxanne and I continually observe the many ways Early Steps has changed classroom instruction. It has created sweeping changes in classroom teaching. It has changed reading instruction in Resource and Title One classrooms. It has created a cohesive environment for learning. Her closing comments provide powerful testimony:

> "I listen more diagnostically than ever before. Early Steps has helped me be far more aware of pacing. This is the most difficult part of teaching. Early Steps has also showed me how all parts of my reading program fit together and how much each part must move forward with the other. Every child must be pushed, but not too hard. Early Steps is the most powerful tool I have obtained since becoming an educator 16 years ago. With this power comes tremendous responsibility. I now believe every child can learn to read if taught appropriately."

References

Adams, M. J. (1990). *Beginning to read: Thinking and learning about print.* Cambridge: The MIT Press.

Anderson, R.C. & Wilson, P.T. & Fielding, L.G. (1988). Growth in reading and how children spend their time outside of school. *Reading Research Quarterly,* 23, 285-303.

Calfee, R. (1991). Decoding and spelling. What to teach and how to teach it. *Psychological Science,* 2, 83-85.

Clarke, L. E. (1988) Invented spelling versus traditional spelling in first graders writings: Effects of learning to spell and read. *Research in the Teaching of English*, 22, 281-309.

Clay, M. (1979) *Reading: the patterning of complex behavior.* Auckland, New Zealand: Heinemann.

Clay, M. (1985). *The early detection of complex behavior.* Auckland, New Zealand: Heinemann.

Cunningham, P. (1975-1976). Investigating a synthesized theory of mediated word identification. *Reading Research Quarterly.* 11, 127-143.

Cunningham, P. (1995). *Phonics they use: words for reading and writing.* New York, NY: Harper Collins.

Dowhower, S.L. (1994). Repeated reading revisited: Research into practice. *Reading and writing Quarterly: Overcoming Learning Difficulties.* 10, 343-358.

Fountas, I. C. & Pinnell, G. S. (1996). *Guided Reading: Good first teaching for all Children.* Ports mouth, NH: Heinemann.

Gambrell, L., Wilson R., & Gantt, W. (1981). Classroom observations of task-attending behaviors of good and poor readers. *Journal of Educational Research*, 74, 400-404.

Goswami, U. (1986). Children's use of analogy in learning to read: A developmental study. *Journal of Experimental Child Pychology.* 452,73-83.

Henderson, E. (1990). *Teaching Spelling.* Boston: Houghton Mifflin Co.

Hoffman, J. & Crone, S. (1984). The oral recitation lesson: A research derived strategy for reading in basal texts. Paper presented at the annual meeting of the National Reading Conference, November 28, 1984, St. Petersburg Beach, Florida.

Johns, J. (1997). *Basic reading inventory: preprimer through grade eight* (5th edition). Dubuque, IA: Kendall/Hunt Co.

Johnson, M. Kress, R. & J. Pikulsky. (1987). *Informal Reading Inventories (2nd ed.).* Newark, DE:

International Reading Association.

Lombardino, Lindo. DeFillip, F., Sarisky, C. & Montgomery, A (1992). Kindergarten children's performance on the Early Screening Instrument. Paper presented at the Annual Convention of the American Speech/Language and Hearing Association, San Antonio, Texas.

Morris, D. (1981). Concept of word: A developmental phenomenon in the beginning reading and writing process. *Language Arts*, 58, 659-668.

Morris, D. (1999). *The Howard Street Tutoring Manual: Teaching at-risk readers in the primary grades*. New York: Guilford Press

Morris. D. (1992). What constitutes at-risk: Screening children for first grade reading intervention. In W. Secord (Ed.) *Best practices in school speech-language pathology*. Vol. 2, pp. 43-51. San Antonio, TX:Psychological Corporation.

Morris, D. (1983). Concept of word and phoneme awareness in the beginning reader. *Research in the Teaching of English*. 17, 359-373.

Morris, D. , & Nelson, L. (1992). Supported oral reading with low-achieving second graders. *Reading Research and Instruction*. 32, 1, 49-63.

Morris, D., Shaw, B., & Perney, J. (1990). Helping low readers in grades 2 and 3: An after school volunteer tutoring program. *Elementary School Journal*, 91, 133-150.

Morris, D. & Perney, J. (1984). Developmental spelling as a predictor of first grade reading achievement. *Elementary School Journal*. 84, 441-457.

Perney, J. & Morris, D. & Carter, (1997). Factorial and predictive validity of first grader's scores on the Early Screening Reading Instrument. *Psychological Reports*, 81, 207-210.

Read, C. (1975). *Children's categorization of speech sounds in English*. Urbana, Ill:NCTE Committee on Research.

Santa, C. & Høien, T. (1999). Early Steps: A program for early intervention of reading problems. *Reading Research Quarterly*. 34, 54-79.

Stauffer, R. (1969). Directing reading maturity as a cognitive process. New York: Harper & Row.

Appendix A:
Early Reading Screening
Instrument

TEACHER MATERIALS

- List of Materials

- ERSI Abbreviated Teacher Directions

- Scoring Guide For Spelling

- Two pencils and a plain 3x5 card

- School or Class Forms

EARLY READING SCREENING INSTRUMENT
List of Materials

One Copy Per Teacher:

Teacher Materials:
>   ERSI Abbreviated Teacher Directions
>   Scoring Guide for spelling
>   Two pencils and a plain *3x5* card.
>   School or Class Forms
>>   First Steps Teacher Rank of Student Reading Expectations
>>   First Steps Screening and Selection: Class Tally

Testing Materials: (The test is divided into two parts for administration at two different times. Giving the entire battery at once is too tiring for a beginning first grader).
>   Part 1:
>   1.1 Alphabet - laminate to the inside cover of a file folder
>   1.2 Concept of Word: Katie Book—photocopy and make into a
>   small book
>   1.3 Basal Words - laminate to the inside cover of file folder

>   Part 2:
>   2.1 Concept of Word: *My Home*
>   "*My Home*", Book (2.1), by June Melser, purchased from the
>   Wright Group, 19201 120th Avenue N.E.
>   Bothell, WA. 98011-9512
>   2.2 List of spelling words (Phonemic Awareness).
>   2.3 Decodable words, Laminate to outside cover of file folder

Student Materials: One copy for each student tested
>   Early Reading Screening Instrument
>   (Score Cover Sheet)
>   Alphabet Writing Sheet (1 .1)
>   Spelling Answer Sheet (2.2)

EARLY READING SCREENING INSTRUMENT
Abbreviated Teacher Directions

1.1   ALPHABET

Recognition

Procedures: Teacher points; child names.

Marking:

Error	Marking	Example
doesn't know	circle	(k)
wrong letter	write above	J over G
self correction	check	m ✓ over n

Scoring: All reversals count as errors. Self-correction: **no** error.

Production

Procedures: Teacher calls out letter, child writes capital **or** lowercase.

Marking: Teacher marks as student writes.
Write errors above letter on score sheet.
Circle if no attempt is made.

Scoring: Left-right reversal counts correct *(b-d)*.
Up-down reversal counts as **error** *(p-d)*.
Sell-correction: **no** error.

1.2   CONCEPT OF WORD ('Katie" book)

Procedures: *Introduce page 1 by asking child, "What does the picture show?"*
1. Teacher finger-point reads page 1.
2. Child finger-point reads page 1.
3. Teacher points to underlined words in numerical order, child identifies.
Proceed to pages 2&3, following above steps on each page.

Marking: Pointing: ✓ or 0   (must read and point correctly to each word; self-corrections count as correct answers.)

Word: ✓ or 0 or write-in incorrect word.

Scoring: Scores on this section are combined with scores on My Home task. See part 2.1, "Scoring" on next page.

1.3   WORD RECOGNITION (Basal Words)

Procedures: Hold card below each word and have child read the word. (**Note**: Stop if no response is given to first four words.)

Marking: ✓ or 0 or write-in incorrect word.

Scoring: Count ✓'s.

2.1   CONCEPT OF WORD (My Home)

Procedures: *Read the title to introduce book. Then have child name the animal pictures on pages 2-5. As pages 6-7 are turned to, teacher covers page 7 with hand. Teacher asks child to predict what the dog and rabbit will do, then reveals page 7. Return to page 2 to begin reading.*

           1.   Teacher finger-point reads page 2.
           2.   Child attempts to finger-point and read page 2.
           3.   Teacher points to word underlined on score sheet for page 2. Child attempts to read it. (Teacher records responses.)

           Follow same procedures on page 3.

           On pages 4, 5, and 7, child reads on his own. On page 4 only, teacher may help if needed by placing child's finger on the word My and saying "my".
    (**Note:** Teacher may read pages 6 & 8 to the child.)

Marking: Same as section **1.2** opposite page.

Scoring: Count ✓'s for pointing in sections 1.2 and 2.1. Enter total for pointing in score box in 2.1 section.

           Count ✓'s for identifying words in sections **1.2 and 2.1.** Enter total for identifying words in score box in 2.1 section.

2.2   PHONEME AWARENESS (Spelling)

Procedures: *Teacher models spelling of sample words (mat, lip) by asking student to think about what letter comes first, what next, and so on. (Teacher writes the words.)*
1.   Teacher gives child the pencil and begins to dictate the 12 words.
2.   Child attempts to spell each word on his own.
3.   Teacher may only help once on words #1 or #2. No helps are given on remaining words. *Teacher observes spelling and may ask student* to *identify letters that are unreadable.*

(**Note: If** the child fails to provide the initial consonant on <u>both</u> the sample words <u>and</u> also each of the two test words, teacher may stop the spelling test.)

Marking :   Teacher copies words as child writes.

Scoring: **See scoring guide.**

2.3   WORD RECOGNITION (Decodable words)

Procedures:
    Marking: ⟩——— Same as section 1.3 above.
    Scoring:

CALCULATING TOTALS			
ALPHABET $\frac{a+b+c}{78}$ x 10 = TOTAL		**PHONEME AWARENESS** $\frac{f}{42}$ x 10 = TOTAL	
CONCEPT OF WORD $\frac{d+e}{16}$ x 10 = TOTAL		**WORD RECOGNITION** $\frac{g+h}{20}$ x 10 = TOTAL	
Round to nearest tenth; .05's round up. Add four TOTALS to calculate GRAND TOTAL.			

SCORING GUIDE FOR SPELLING

EARLY READING SCREENING INSTRUMENT
SECTION 2.2 PHONEME AWARENESS

One point is awarded for each phoneme represented by an appropriate letter. Examiners will need to interpret spellings if no example below matches child's attempt. Phoneme's represented out of order are not awarded points. Note maximum points per word varies from 3 to 4.

Points		1	2	3	4
1	back	B, BN	BC, BK, BA, BAE BIG, BOC	BAC, BAK, BAKE, BACK	
2	feet	F, FA	FT, FE, FIT	FET, FEAT, FETE, FEET	
3	step	S, C, SOT	ST, CP, SA, SE	STP, SAP, CAP, CAP, STIP	STAP, STEP
4	junk	J, G	JK, GC, JO, GU	JOK, GOK, GNK, JIJK	JONG, GUNK
5	picking	P, P0	PK, PC, PE, PN	PEC, PEK, P1K, PEN, PKN	PECN, PICEN, PEKN, PICKING
6	mail	M, MI	ML. MA, MAO, ME	MAL, MAOL, MALE, MEL, MAIL	
7	side	5, C, ST	SE, CD, SA, SED	SID, CID, SAD, SOD, SIDE	
8	chin	G, J, H	GN, IN, HN, GAN	GEN, HIN, CHEN, CHIN	
9	dress	D, J, G	JS, GS, DOS	JAS, DES, IRS, DRS, DESS, GAS	DRAS, JRES, DRES, DRESS
10	peeked	P	PT, PE, PK, KIT	PET, PCT, PEK, PIKT, PEET	PECT, PEKED, PEEKT, PEEKED
11	lamp	L	LP, LA, LOP, LM	LAP, LAPE, LAM, LMP	LAMPE, LAMP
12	road	R, W, RT	RD. RO	ROD, ROED, RODE, ROAD	

* printed with permission of Darrell Morris

SCHOOL _____ TEACHER _____ DATE _____

SCREENING SCORES - ERSI

NAME	ALPHABET				CONCEPT OF WORD			PHONEME AWARENESS		WORD RECOGNITION			GRAND TOTAL	Teacher Rank
	Up 26	Low 26	Prod. 26	TOTAL	Point 8	Word 8	TOTAL	Count 42	TOTAL	Bas 10	Dec 10	TOTAL		

TESTING MATERIALS

Part 1:

- 1.1 Alphabet - laminate to the inside cover of a file folder

- 1.2 Concept of Word: Katie Book - photocopy and make into a small book

- 1.3 Basal Words - laminate to the inside cover of file folder

Part 2:

- 2.1 Concept of Word: *"My Home"*. by June Melser, purchased from the Wright Group, 19201 120th Avenue N.E. Bothell, WA. 98011-9512

- 2.3 Decodable Words - laminate to outside cover of file folder

EARLY READING SCREENING INSTRUMENT

FOLDER INCLUDES:
Alphabet (1.1)
Basal Words (1.3)
Decodable Words (2.3)

(For convenience, other ERSI materials may also be stored in this folder.)

Cut out for screening folder cover.

EARLY READING SCREENING INSTRUMENT (ERSI)

Cut out for screening folder tab.

1.1 Alphabet Recognition and Production

A	F	K	P	W	Z
B	H	O	J	U	
C	Y	L	Q	M	
D	N	S	X	I	
E	G	R	V	T	

---

a	f	k	p	w	z
b	h	o	j	u	
c	y	l	q	m	
d	n	s	x	i	
e	g	r	v	t	

Kate is walking in the rain.

She sees a big dog.

The dog shakes water on Katie.

BASAL WORDS

1. is

2. come

3. good

4. here

5. like

6. and

7. mother

8. make

9. work

10. day

My Home

by June Melser CHAPTER .1

"My home is here," said the bird.

2

"My home is here," said the frog.

3

"My home is here," said the pig.

4

"My home is here,"
said the dog.

5

A dog!

A rabbit!

6

"My home is here,"
said the rabbit.

7

Come back, rabbit!

8

DECODABLE WORDS

1. cap

2. net

3. win

4. bug

5. fat

6. mop

7. led

8. dig

9. job

10. mud

STUDENT MATERIALS

- Individual Score Sheet

- Alphabet Writing Sheet

- Spelling Answer Sheet

EARLY READING SCREENING
INSTRUMENT
Individual Score Sheet

School——————————— Student Name —————————

Examiner——————————— Classroom Teacher —————————

Date———————————

ALPHABET				CONCEPT OF WORD			PH. AWARE.		WORD REC.		
Up	Low	Prod.		Point	Word		Count		Bas	Dec	
26	26	26	TOTAL	8	8	TOTAL	42	TOTAL	10	10	TOTAL
__	__	__	(__)	__	__	(__)	__	(__)	__	__	(__)
(a)	(b)	(c)		(d)	(e)		(f)		(g)	(h)	

GRAND
TOTAL

1.1 ALPHABET

RECOGNITION: A F K P W Z   B H O J U   C Y L Q M

D N S X I   E G R V T

a f k p w z   b h o j u   c y l q m

d n s x i   e g r v t

CORRECT ____/26
(a)

CORRECT ____/26
(b)

PRODUCTION: A F K P W Z   B H O J U   C Y L Q M

D N S X I   E G R V T

CORRECT ____/26
(c)

1.2 CONCEPT OF WORD ("Katie" Book)

	Point	Words

1. Katie is <u>walking</u> in the <u>rain</u>. ———— 1 ———— 2 ————

2. <u>She</u> sees a <u>big</u> dog. ———— 1 ———— 2 ————

3. The <u>dog</u> shakes <u>water</u> on Katie. ———— 1 ———— 2 ————

> Scores are combined with section 2.1. When test is completed, count ✓'s for pointing & words. Record in box in section 2.1.

1.3 WORD RECOGNITION (Basal Words)

1. is ————   4. here ————   7. mother ————   10. day ————

2. come ————   5. like ————   8. make ————

3. good ————   6. and ————   9. work ————

> # CORRECT
> ___ /10
> (g)

2.1 CONCEPT OF WORD (My Home)

Page	Point	Word

(2) "My home is <u>here</u>," ————   ————
said the bird.

(3) "My home <u>is</u> here," ————   ————
said the frog.

(4) "My home is here," ————
said the pig.

(5) "My home is here," ————
said the dog.

(7) "My home is here", ————
said the rabbit.

> Note: Count ✓'s for pointing & words from sections 1.2 and 2.1 and record totals below.
>
> # CORRECT (point)___/8
> (d)
> # CORRECT (point)___/8
> (e)

2 PHONEMIC AWARENESS (Spelling)

1. back _____
2. feet _____
3. step _____
4. junk _____
5. picking _____
6. mail _____
7. side _____
8. chin _____
9. dress _____
10. peeked _____
11. lamp _____
12. road _____

POINTS_____/42
(f)

2.3 WORD RECOGNITION (Decodable)

1. cap _____
2. net _____
3. win _____
4. bug _____
5. fat _____
6. mop _____
7. led _____
8. dig _____
9. job _____
10. mud _____

CORRECT_____/ 10
(h)

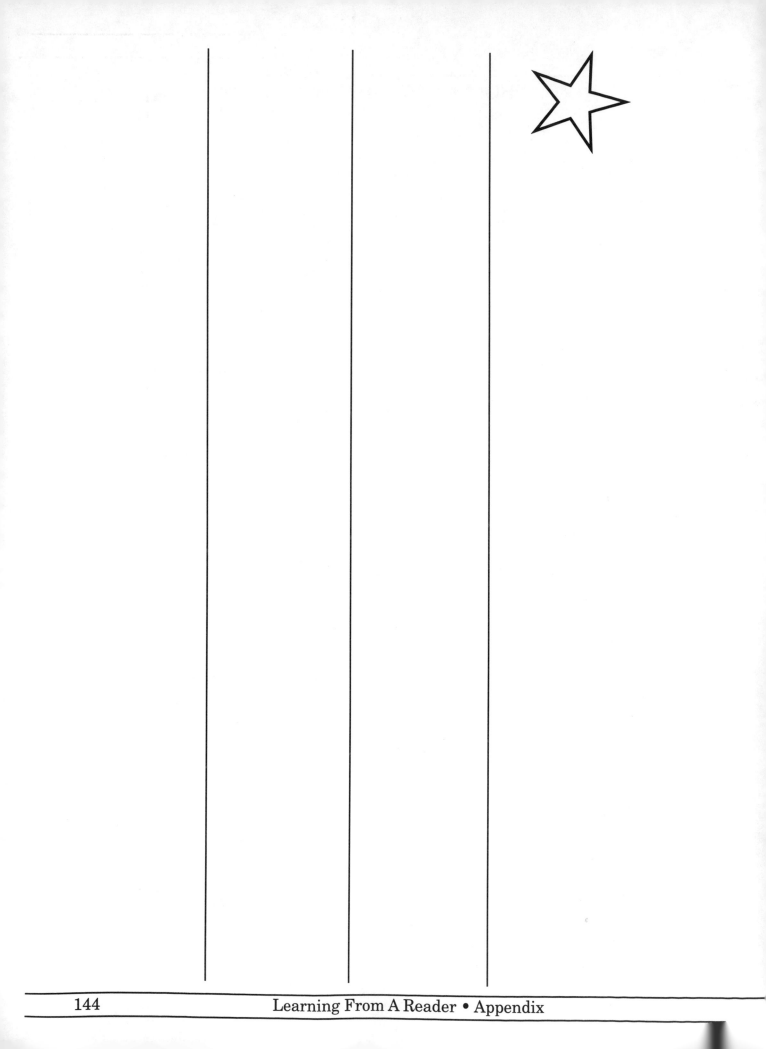

Name_____

1. _____

2. _____

3. _____

4. _____

5. _____

6. _____

7. _____

8. _____

9. _____

10. _____

11. _____

12. _____

Appendix B

Early Steps Books

LEVEL 1

_____Birthday Cake
_____Chocolate Cake
_____Dinner
_____Farm
_____Go, Go, Go.
_____I want Ice Cream
_____Little Brother
_____My Puppy
_____Party, A
_____Picnic
_____Who's Going to Lick the Bowl?

LEVEL 2

_____Bee
_____Bicycle
_____Big Hill
_____Clown and Elephant
_____Feet
_____Flying
_____Ghost
_____House Cleaning
_____If you Meet a Dragon
_____In the Mirror
_____Major Jump
_____Painting
_____Storm
_____Tree House
_____Who lives Here?
_____Yak Soup

LEVEL 3

_____Come With Me
_____Frightened
_____I Am a Bookworm
_____I Can Jump
_____I Can Paint
_____I Love My family
_____Ice Cream
_____Like Me
_____Little Brother
_____Little Pig
_____Long, Long Tail
_____Monster Sandwich
_____Mouse
_____My Home (Dog)
_____My Home (Turtle)
_____My Little Mouse
_____My Shadow
_____Nighttime
_____On a Chair
_____One, One is the Sun
_____Our Granny
_____Our Street
_____Pat, Pat, Pat

_____Plop
_____Race
_____Round and Round
_____Shoo
_____Snap
_____Splash
_____Stop
_____What is a Huggles?
_____What's for Lunch?
_____When Itchy Witchy Sneezes
_____Where Are They Going?
_____Whose Birthday Is It Today?

LEVEL 4

_____Big and Little
_____Bus Ride
_____Buzzing Flies
_____Cave
_____Dabbling in Dough
_____Copycat
_____Dan, The Flying Man
_____Danger
_____Dressing-Up Box
_____Farm Concert
_____Friends, The
_____Frogs Can Jump
_____Going to School
_____Hello
_____Houses
_____Hug is Warm
_____Joshua James Likes Trucks
_____Monster's Party
_____Mosquito
_____My Home
_____No, No
_____Scat! Said the Cat
_____Shark in a Sack
_____Shoes
_____Silly Old Possum
_____Sleeping Out
_____Ssssh!
_____Tails
_____To New York
_____Two Little Dogs
_____Uncle Buncle's House
_____Up in a Tree
_____What a Mess
_____Who Wants to Live in My House?

LEVEL 5

_____Banana Shake
_____Cats and Kittens
_____Fluffy Chicks
_____Good for You

_____Goodbye, Lucy
_____Hairy Bear
_____Haunted House
_____Horace
_____I'm Bigger than You
_____In a Dark, Dark Wood
_____Mrs. Wishy-Washy
_____Night Train
_____Pumpkin
_____Rain in the Hills
_____Rum Tum Tum
_____Snow
_____Spider, Spider
_____These Are My Pets
_____Three Little Ducks
_____Too Big for Me
_____Wake Up, Mom
_____What Shall I Wear?
_____What Would You Like?
_____Where is Baby Tom?
_____Who Are You?
_____Woosh!
_____Yum and Yuck

LEVEL 6

_____Along Comes Jake
_____Beach
_____Big Toe
_____Boo-Hoo
_____Dreams
_____Grumpy Elephant
_____Hot Rod Harry
_____I'm Looking for My Hat
_____Jigaree
_____Joe's Father
_____Let's Have a Swim
_____Little Sister's Birthday
_____Lump in My Bed
_____Monkey Bridge
_____Mr. Grump
_____My Great, Big Brother
_____Obadiah
_____Oh, Jump in a Sack
_____One Cold, Wet Night
_____Poor Old Polly
_____Seed
_____Sing a Song
_____Staying Overnight
_____Ten Little Bears
_____Too Many Balloons
_____Victor Makes a TV
_____Who is Coming?
_____Who Is Who?

LEVEL 7

_____All By Myself
_____Baked Potato
_____Birthday Cake
_____Bread
_____Camping Outside
_____Come for a Swim
_____Donkey in the Lion's Skin
_____Don't Panic
_____Find a Caterpillar

_____Fizz and Splutter
_____Go, Dog, Go
_____Grandpa, Grandpa
_____Jennifer Pockets
_____Just Like Me
_____Lazy Mary
_____Listen to Me
_____Red Rose
_____Smarty Pants
_____Staying Overnight
_____This is my House
_____This is my School
_____Time for School, Little Dinosaur
_____Wait Skates
_____Who Will be My Mother?
_____Yes, Ma'am

LEVEL 8

_____Are You My Mother?
_____Birthday Book
_____Boy and the Wolf,
_____Don't You Laugh at Me
_____Dry and Snug and Warm
_____Fox and the Crow
_____Goose that Laid the Golden Egg
_____Hare and the Tortoise
_____Hungry Giant
_____Hungry Monster
_____Just Go to Bed
_____Katie Couldn't
_____Katie Did It
_____Lion and the Mouse
_____Make a Boat that Floats
_____Meanies
_____Paul the Pitcher
_____Taking Jason To Grandma's
_____This is My Friend
_____To Town
_____Wet Grass
_____What a Bad Dream
_____When I Get Bigger
_____Where Are You Going, Aja Rose?
_____Wind Blows Strong

LEVEL 9

_____Bear and Two Friends
_____Boy Who Cried Wolf
_____Catch that Frog
_____Circus Book
_____Donkey and the Lapdog
_____Donkey in the Pond
_____Dragon
_____Ducks and the Tortoise
_____Eagle and the Man
_____Farmer and His Sons
_____Great Big Enormous Turnip
_____Happy Faces
_____I Just Forgot
_____I Was So Mad
_____Just Grandma and Me
_____Just Grandpa and Me
_____Just Me and My Cousin
_____Just Me and My Dad
_____Just Me and My Puppy

_____Just My friend and Me
_____Just Shopping with Mom
_____Lion's Tail
_____Man, His Son, and the Donkey
_____Merry Christmas, Mom and Dad
_____Mother Hen
_____Pat's New Puppy
_____Roly-Poly
_____Spaghetti, Spaghetti
_____Teeny Tiny Woman
_____Tiger is a Scaredy Cat
_____To Market, To Market
_____Who Will be My Friends?

*In "Little Critter Read It Yourself
Storybook" 6 stories

END OF YEAR ASSESSMENT

Daniel's Duck
Frog and Toad All Year
Look For Me
Mouse Tales
Storm
Wild, Wild Wolves

LEVEL 10

_____Abracadabra
_____Barney's Horse
_____Bird Table
_____Boy and the Lion
_____Cave Boy
_____Chester
_____Danny and the Dinosaur
_____Hello House
_____Help Me
_____Horse in Harry's Room
_____Just a Daydream
_____Katie Can
_____Kiss for Little Bear
_____Let Me In
_____Little Bear
_____Little Knight
_____Loose Laces
_____Missing Necklace
_____Mouse Tales
_____My New Boy
_____Popcorn Book
_____Pot of Gold
_____Red and Blue Mittens
_____Red Fox and His Canoe
_____Sammy's supper
_____So sick
_____Tents
_____Three Little Pigs
_____Toads Eat Out
_____Town Mouse and Country Mouse
_____Who's Afraid of the Dark?
_____Wiggly Jiggly Line

LEVEL 11

_____Henry's Choice
_____Kick, Pass, and Run
_____Lizards, and Salamanders
_____Monkey and the Fisherman
_____Mouse Soup
_____Mystery Seeds
_____Owl at Home
_____Sick Lion
_____Sir Small and the Dragonfly
_____Slim, Shorty, and the Mule

Materials and Supplies
Books

Essentials:

The following books and book sets are needed to assure enough varied material on each of the twelve Early Steps book levels. One set of books can be used for three or four children; however, an extra set will prove very convenient and will allow children to take books home regularly. (The prices may not be accurate. Many will have changed since printing these lists.)

Story Box Level I

Catalogue#	Title	Price	Source
215459	Sets A-G	170.70	The Wright Group
211925	Read Together Set A	33.40	19201 120th Avenue NE
212174	Read Together Set B	33.40	Bothell, WA 98011-9
212425	Read Together Set C	33.40	800-523-2371

(estimated prices)

Sunshine Books

340708	Set B	$22.90
340716	Set C	$22.90
340724	Set D	$22.90
340856	Set E	$33.40
340864	Set F	$33.40

(estimated prices)

Fables **From Aesop**

34997	Complete Set	$69.60

(estimated prices)

Reading Unlimited
Level 2 (Pupil booklets)
#0-673 10606-3 $22.00
Level 3 (Pupil booklets)
#0-673-10616-0 $22.00
Level 4 (Pupil booklets)
#0-673-10626-8 $22.00

(estimated prices)

Scott Foresman
P.O. Box 450129
Atlanta, GA 30345
800-554-4411

Step Into Reading - Step 1   Random House, Inc. (Selected paperbacks)
400 Flahn Road
Westminister, MD 21157
800-733-3000

0394-89571-2	Cave Boy	$3.99
0394-88864-2	Hello House	$3.99
0394-88277-6	My New Boy	$3.99
0394-89625-4	Sir Small and the Dragonfly	$3.99
0394-88320-9	Teeny Tiny Woman	$3.99
0394-88056-0	Tiger is a Scaredy Cat	$3.99

(estimated prices)

Picture Back Readers

0-679-80789-6	Time for School, Little Dinosaur	$2.25

(estimated prices)

Beginner Books

0-394-80018-4	Are You My Mother?	$7.99
0-394-80020-6	Go, Dog, Go	$7.99

(estimated prices)

Rookie Readers   **Children's Press**
5440 North Cumberland
Chicago, IL 60656

0-516-43493-4	Hot Rod Harry	$3.50
0-516-43525-6	Joshua James.. Trucks	$3.50
0-51 6-42047-X	Just Like Me	$3.50
0-516-42082-8	Katie Can	$3.50
0-516-42069-0	Katie Couldn't	$3.50
0-516-42043-7	Katie Did It	$3.50
0-516-42072-0	Listen To Me	$3.50
0-51 6-42064-X	Paul the Pitcher	$3.50
0-516-42039-9	Wait Skates	$3.50
0-516-42073-9	Who is Coming	$3.50
0-516-42042-9	Who is Who	$3.50
0-516-43633-3	Too Many Balloons	$3.50

(estimated prices)

Harper I Can Read Books   **Harper & Row**
Keystone Industrial Park
Scranton, PA 18512
800-242-7737

0-06-444075-3	Red Fox and His Canoe	$3.75
0-06-444071-0	Who's Afraid of the Dark	$3.75
0-06-444142-3	Barney's House	$3.75
0-06-444095-8	Chester	$3.75
0-06-444002-8	Danny & the Dinosaur	$3.75

(estimated prices)

0-06-444073-7	Horse in Harry's Room	$3.75
0-06-444072-9	Who Will Be My Friends?	$3.75
0-06-444210-7	Kick, Pass, and Run	$3.75
0-06-444041-9	Mouse Soup	$3.75
0-06-444013-3	Mouse Tales	$3.75
0-06-444034-6	Owl at Home	$3.75
0-06-444050-8	Kiss for Little Bear	$3.75
0-06-444004-4	Little Bear	$3.75

(estimated prices)

Mercer Mayer Books　　　　　　　**Donovan Music and Toy**
254 W. Main Street
Waukesha, WI 53186
414-544-1661

11839	Just Me and My Dad	$1.99
11893	Just Grandma and Me	$1.99
11936	Just Grandpa and Me	$1.99
11937	Just Me and My Puppy	$1.99
11938	All By Myself	$1.99
11939	I Was So Mad	$1.99
11941	Me, Too	$1.99
11946	Just Me and My Sister	$1.99
11947	Just My Friend and Me	$1.99
11838	Just For You	$1.99
11943	When I Get Bigger	$1.99
11945	Just Me and My Babysitter	$1.99
11948	Just A Mess	$1.99
11975	I Just Forgot	$1.99
11386	Merry Christmas and My Dad	$1.99

Golden Easy Readers by Mercer Mayer

(estimated prices)

Critter, Read to Yourself　　　　　　　　　　$15.95
(sold as one hard copy book that contains the following books)
This is My School　　This is My House　　These are My Pets
This is My Friend　　The Trip　　Staying Overnight

_____Optional

Recommended Books

The books below are useful but not essential. If the children have been exposed to most of the Story Box and Sunshine books in the classroom, these books will provide some new material. A number of schools have acquired these books in the second year of Early Steps implementation.

Book Bank　　　　　　　　　　　　　　　The Wright Group

#11026	Book Bank complete Set #1	$119.00
#13005	Book Bank complete Set #2	$119.00

(estimated prices)

Early Steps End-Of-Year Assessment
Ordering Information for Books

One of each of the following books should be available for each examiner. As noted, some books are already included in the Early Steps book sets ordered earlier. *Four of the books will need to be ordered.

The Wright Group   Telephone: 800-523-2371
19201 120th Avenue NE
Bothell, WA 98011-9512

#826   The Storm (available only in 6 packs) $17.20
#860   *Look for Me (available only 6 packs) $17.20
                                                (estimated prices)

Harper-Collins   Telephone: 800-242-7737
Keystone Industrial Park
Scranton, PA 18512

0-06-444013-3   Mouse Tales $3.75
0-06-444059-1   *Frog and Toad All Year $3.75
0-06-444031-1   *Daniel's Duck $3.75
                                        (estimated prices)

Random House, Inc.   Telephone: 800-733-3000
400 Hahn Road
Westminister, MD 21157

0-679-81052-8   Wild, Wild Wolves $3.99
                                        (estimated prices)

Appendix C
Word Study Materials

- Letter cards   153-155

- Picture and letter cards   156-170

- Word sort cards   171-217

Duplicating Instructions:

- Copy on tag

- Laminate

- Cut apart into cards

* Permission of printing of picture cards granted by
Kendall/Hunt Publishing Co. • Dubuque, Iowa.

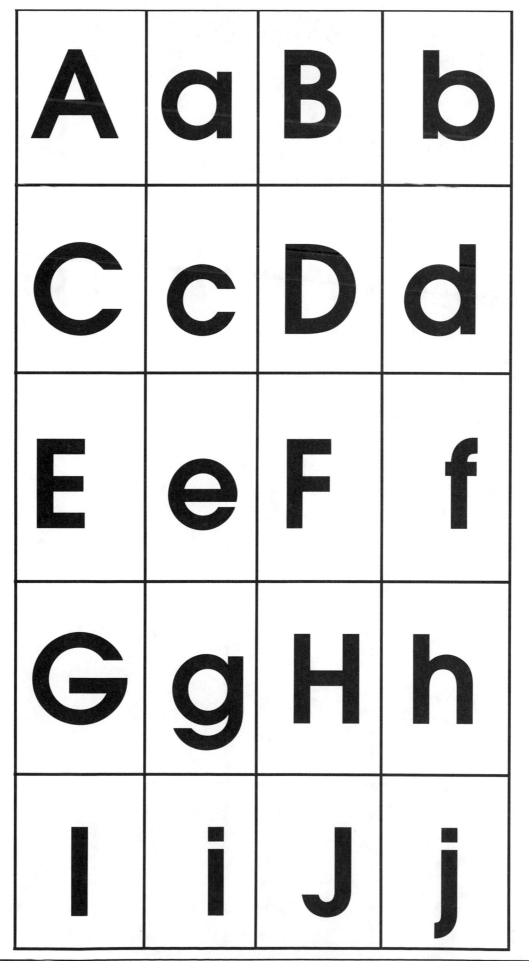

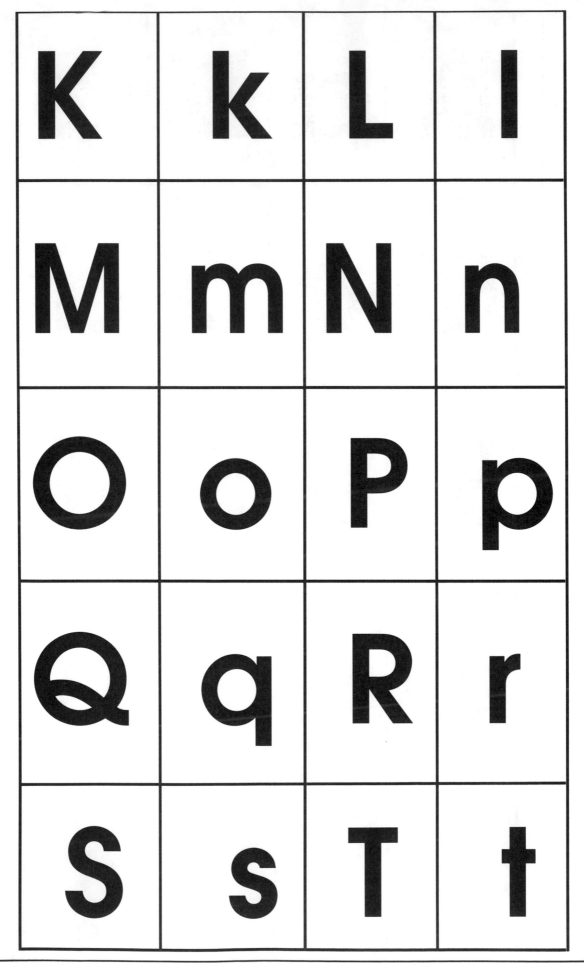

K k	L l
M m	N n
O o	P p
Q q	R r
S s	T t

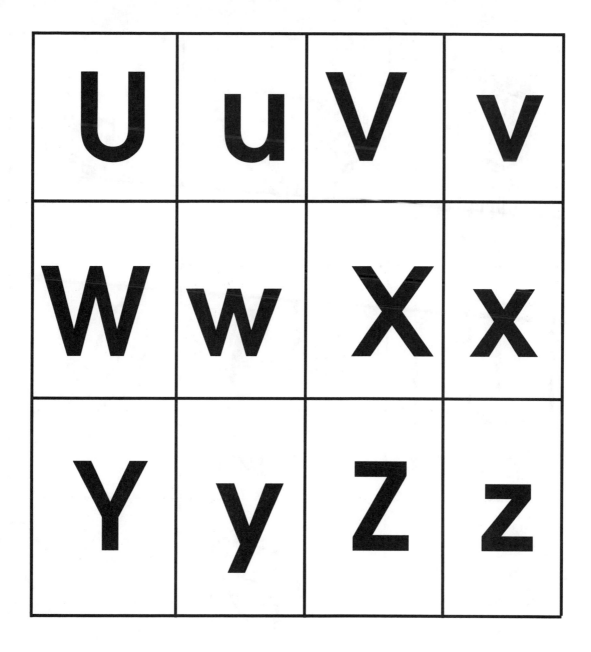

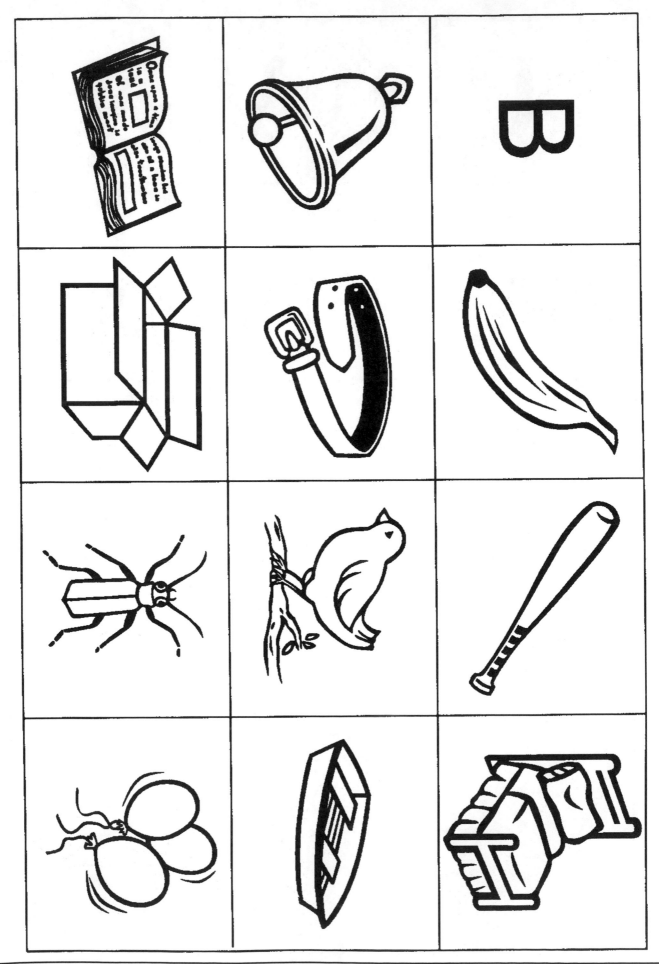

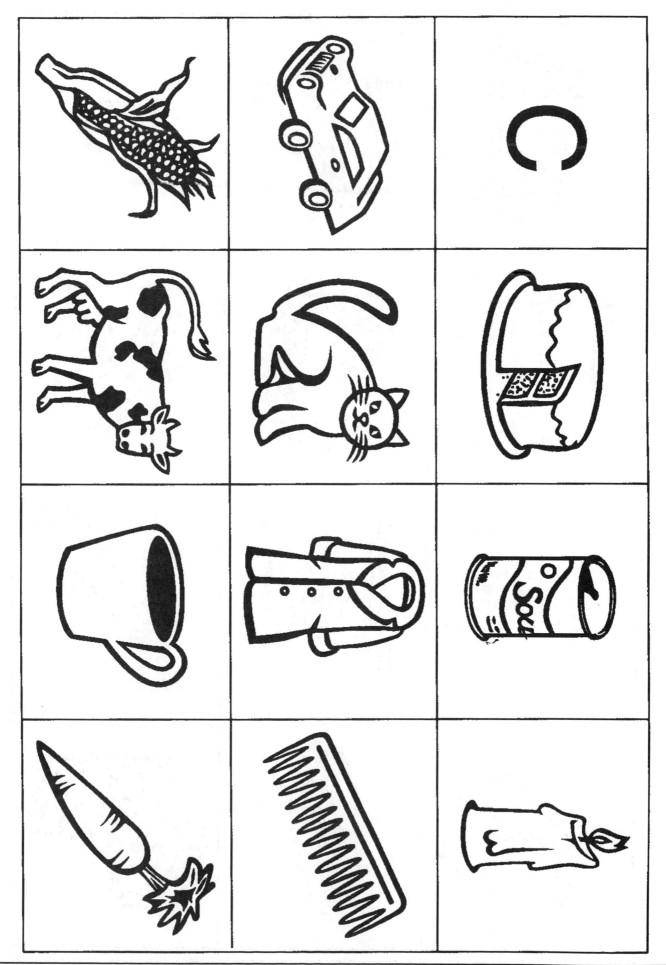

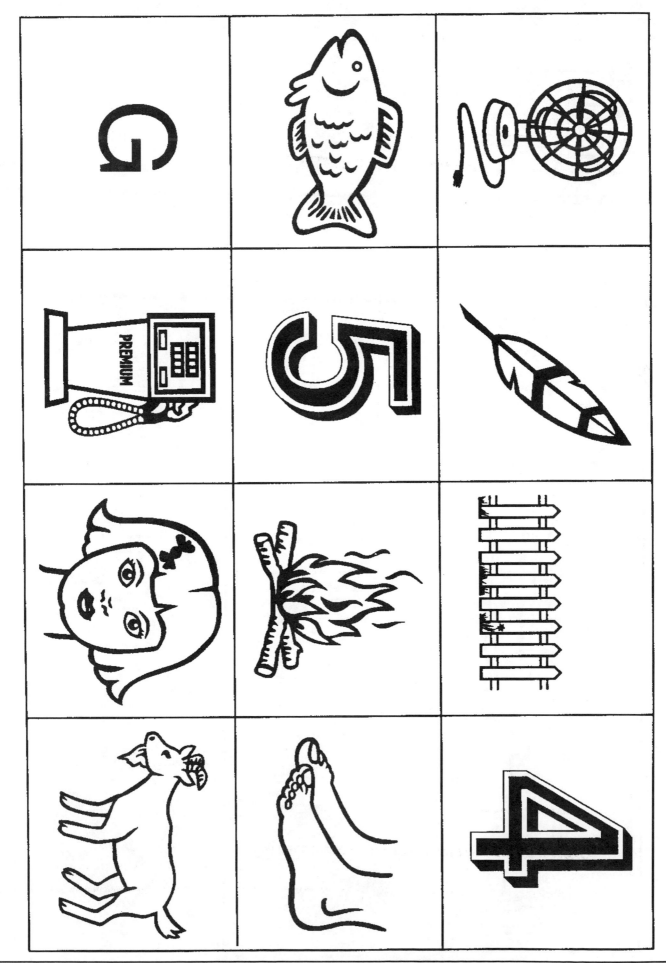

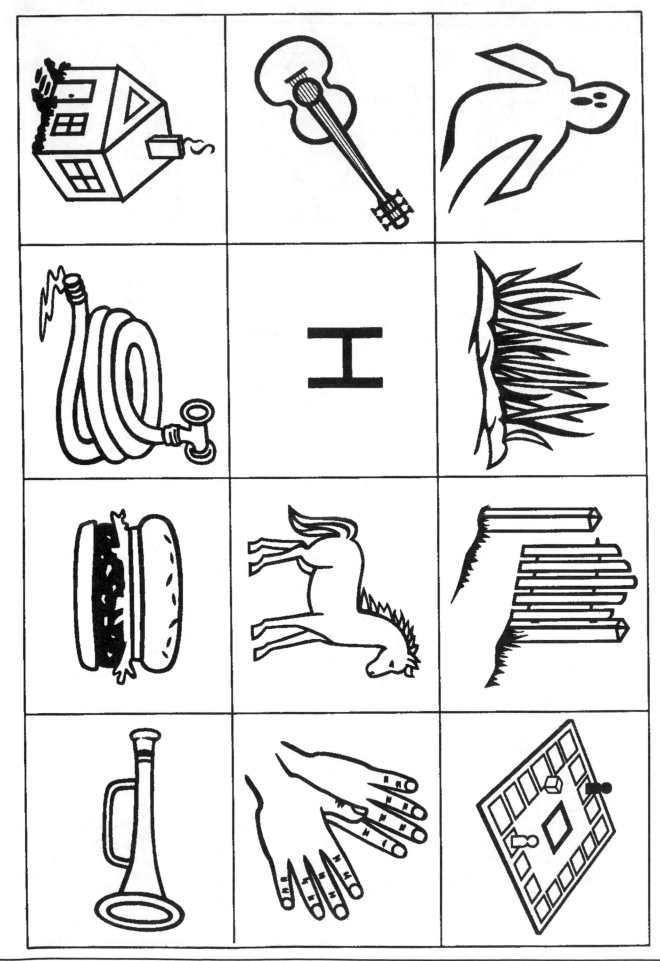

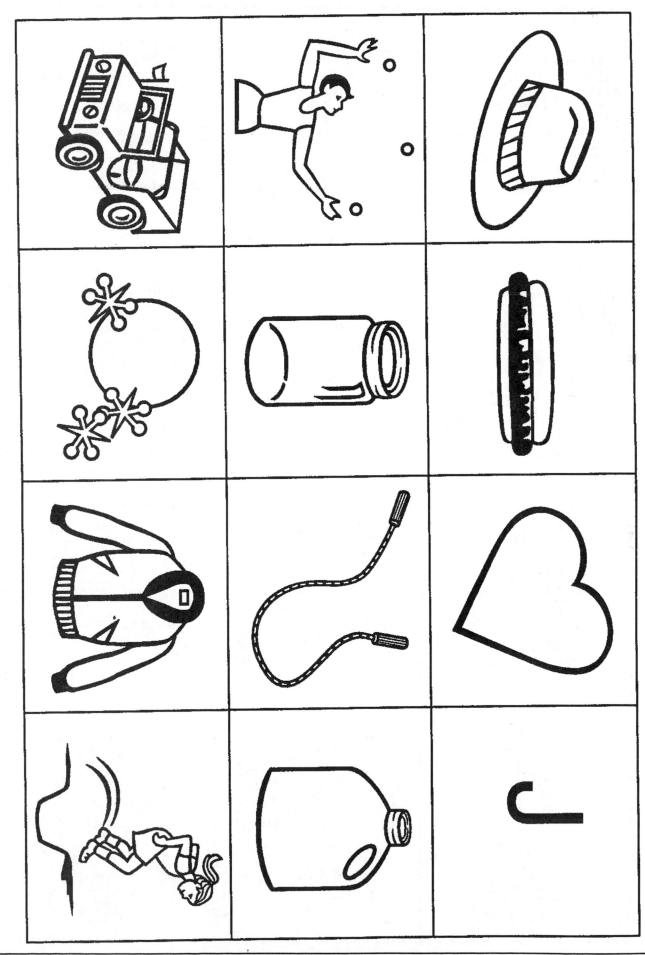

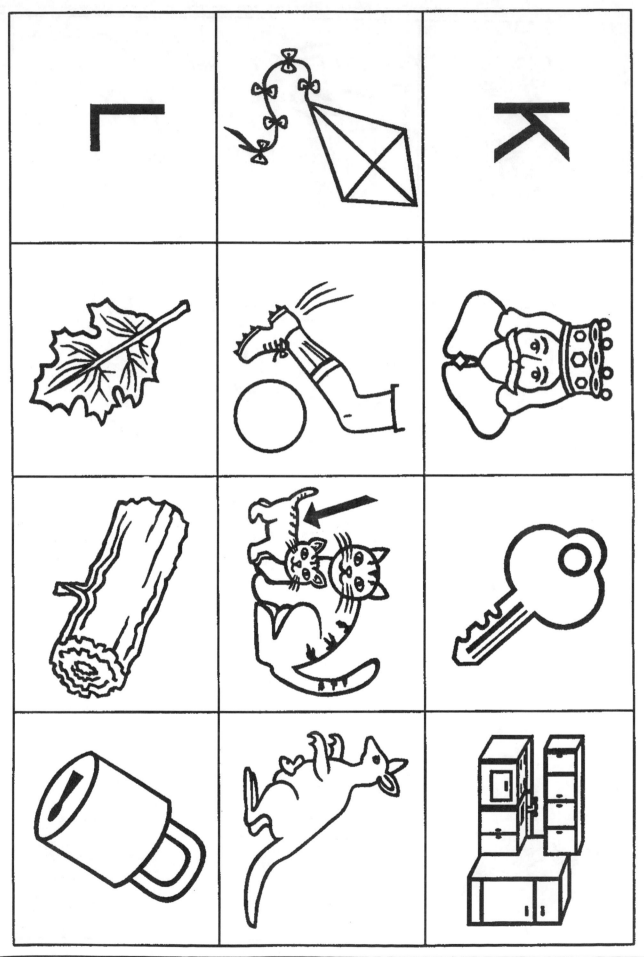

Learning From A Reader • Appendix

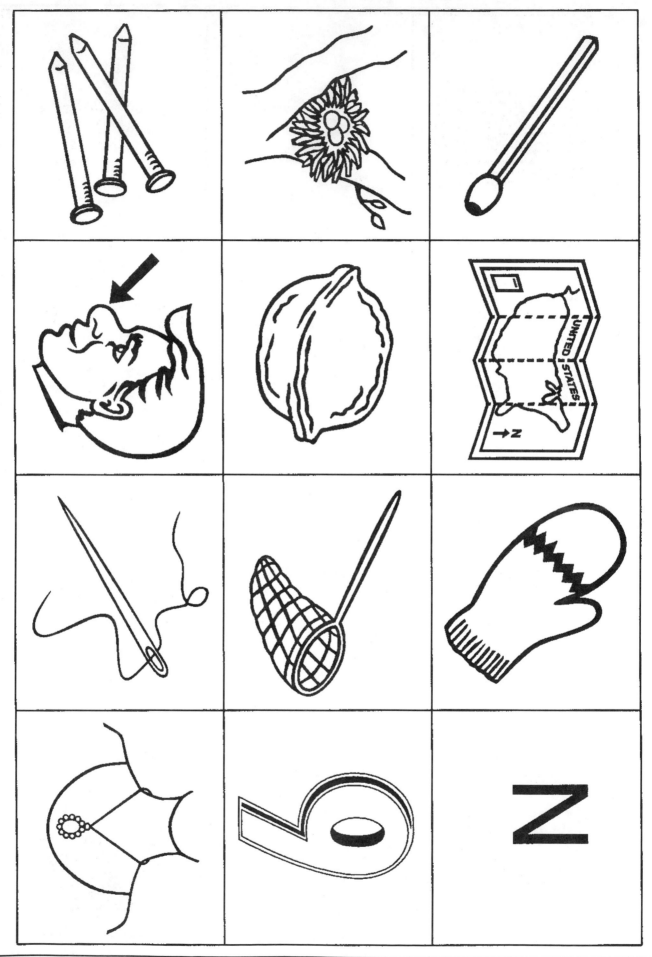

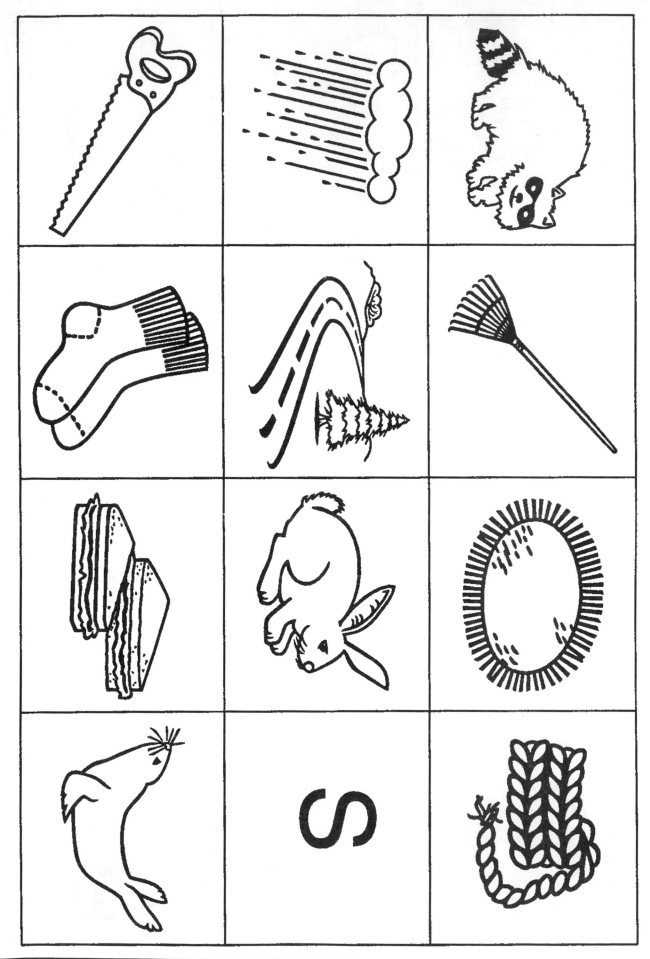

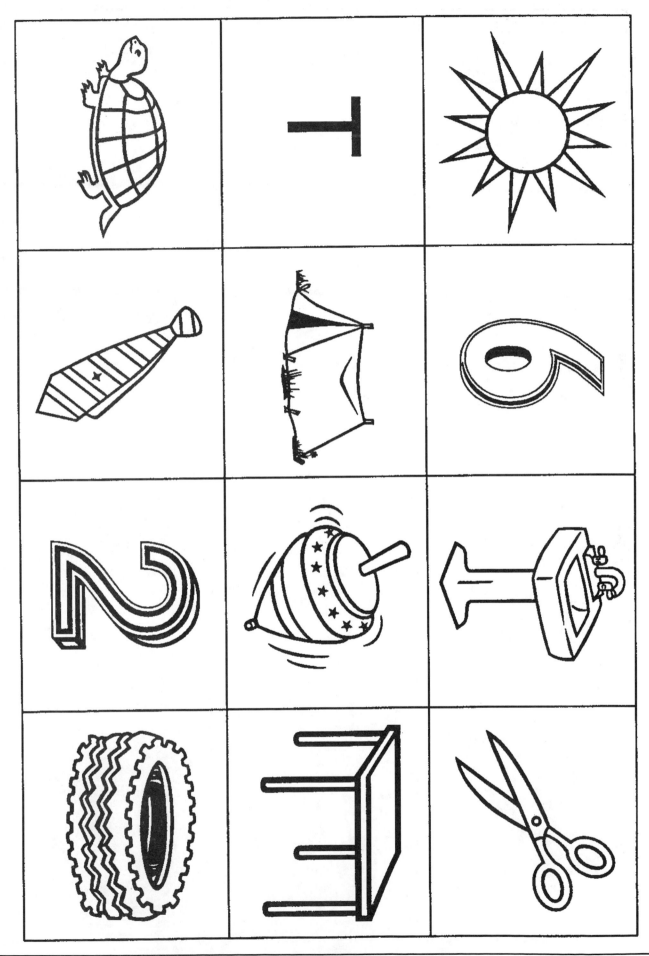

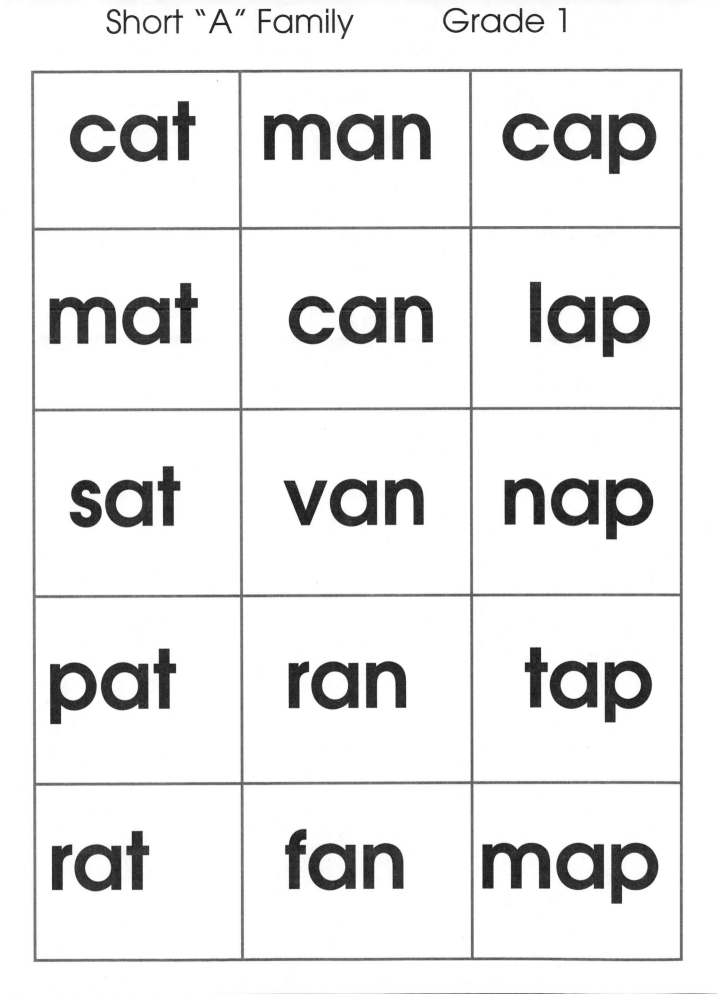

cat	man	cap
mat	can	lap
sat	van	nap
pat	ran	tap
rat	fan	map

flat	pan	sap
hat	plan	clap
	tan	snap

sack	black	
tack	track	
rack	snack	
back		
pack		

hit	big	win
sit	fig	tin
fit	wig	pin
pit	dig	kin
kit	pig	fin

bit	twig	thin
chin		
spin		
skin		

sick	trick	
kick	brick	
lick	stick	
pick	thick	
tick		

hot	top	sock
pot	pop	rock
lot	cop	lock
not	hop	block
got	mop	clock

dot	stop	knock
spot	drop	
	chop	

look	shook	
book		
took		
cook		
hook		

pet	red	hen
net	led	pen
set	bed	men
met	fed	ten
wet	shed	then

Short "E" Family   Grade 1

let	sled	when
jet		

tell	**shell**	
sell	**smell**	
fell		
well		
bell		

cut	bug	run
nut	hug	gun
but	dug	fun
hut	rug	sun
shut	jug	spun

slug	bun	
mug		
plug		

Short "U" Family   Grade 1

duck	tuck	
luck	buck	
suck	cluck	
stuck		
truck		

bad	pig	mom
hat	win	hot
ran	hit	job
map	lip	top
mad	kid	hop

back	his	fox
had	sick	doll
has	this	rock

bus	**bug**	
cup	**but**	
nut	**luck**	
fun		
cut		

that	ship	chop
clap	with	stop
glad		drop

shut		
truck		
must		

pet	web	then
bed	tell	when
let	less	sled
red	sell	

jam	lake	park
ran	race	car
dad	tape	hard
hat	page	barn
cab	same	jar

map	make	card
cat	name	far
flat	take	part
clap	gave	farm

day	clay	
say	stay	
may	play	
way	stray	
pay		

rain	chain	fall
mail	paint	ball
wait	maid	tall
pain	sail	call
tail	paid	wall

small		
mall		
hall		

Vowel Pattern - I

hid	ride	girl
lip	nice	dirt
win	bike	bird
big	five	sir
kick	mile	first

Vowel Pattern - I

hit	side	firm
pin	drive	shirt
swim	dime	third

right	high	
night	flight	
light	tight	
might		
bright		

dot	rope	go
job	note	no
pot	hole	so
mom	nose	
top	coke	

drop	hope	for
jog	bone	corn
lock	code	fork
		born
		fort

horn		
pork		
torn		

stop	woke	
bomb	stone	
shock	spoke	

boat	book	told
road	good	cold
soap	foot	colt
load	look	gold
coal	stood	mold

Learning From A Reader • Appendix

loaf	hook	fold
soak	brook	sold
coach	wood	hold

moon	shoot	toast
roof	tooth	float
pool	broom	cloak
boot		
tool		

boil	spoil	
coin	voice	
soil	boy	
point	toy	
noise		

ten	feet	herd
red	deep	germ
beg	meet	clerk
get	feel	nerve

Learning From A Reader • Appendix

he	bell	free
we	less	green
she	nest	seed
me	left	need
be	pet	bleed

step	queen	serve
sled	jeep	herd

meat	head	
team	lead	
lead	dead	

mean	bread	beach
peak	deaf	leaf
clean	breath	
beat	spread	
dream	sweat	

mud	cute	hurt
cup	rule	burn
bus	use	curl
fun	rude	fur
rug	tune	turn

blue	new	
true	grew	
flue	few	
clue	chew	
sue	screw	

fit	wise	
chin	shine	
this	slide	
	life	

wild	by	mild
mind	my	blind
find	fly	grind
climb	cry	child
kind	sky	

fry		
shy		
spy		
try		

Appendix D:
End-of-Year Assessment

EARLY STEPS END-OF-YEAR ASSESSMENT
CONTENTS

Permission for printing End of Year Assessment granted by Dowell Morris

EARLY STEPS END-OF-YEAR ASSESSMENT
ORDERING INFORMATION FOR BOOKS

One of each of the following books should be available for each examiner. As noted, some books are already included in the First Steps book sets ordered earlier. Two of the books will need to be ordered.

SOURCE: The Wright Group   Telephone: 800-523-2371
19201 120th Avenue NE
Bothell, WA 98011-9512

Catalog No. Title		Unit Price
826	* The Storm (available only in six packs)	$15.60
860	* Look for Me (available only in six packs)	$15.60

SOURCE: Harper Collins   Telephone: 800-242-7737
Keystone Industrial Park
Scanton, PA 18512

Catalog No. Title		Unit Price
0-06-444013-3	*Mouse Tales	$3.50
0-06-444059-1	Frog and Toad All Year	$3.50
0-06-444031-1	Daniel's Duck	$3.50

SOURCE: Random House, Inc.   Telephone: 800-733-3000
400 Hahn Road
Westminister, MD 21157

Catalog No. Title		Unit Price
0-679-81052-8	Wild, Wild Wolves	$3.50

* These books should be in Early Steps book sets purchased earlier and may not need to be ordered unless additional copies are needed.

EARLY STEPS END-OF-YEAR ASSESSMENT
MATERIALS NEEDED

Examiner materials

1. Early Steps End-of-Year Assessment Instructions
2. Word Recognition List (laminated for student to read from)
3. Set of books used for reading passages (or copies of passages):

Emergent	The Storm
Pre primer	Look for Me
Primer	Mouse Tales
1-2	Frog and Toad All Year
2-1	Daniel's Duck
2-2	WIld, WIld Wolves

4. Tape recorder
5. Watch with second hand or stop watch
6. Calculator
7. Blank audio cassette tapes (1 per 5 students)
8. Large clasp envelopes (1 per 5 students)
9. Pencils (at least 2)
10. Index cards (2)

Materials needed for each student

Summary Score Sheet
Spelling Sheet (student writes on)
Passage Reading Score Sheets

EARLY STEPS END-OF-YEAR ASSESSMENT

EXAMINER INSTRUCTIONS

WORD RECOGNITION

1. Student reads words in order

2. Stop if 7 consecutive words are missed.

3 Marking and scoring

    A.   Leave blank if correct.
    B.   Mark 0 for no response.
    C.   Write-in incorrect response.
    D.   Self-corrections marked with ✓ . Count as correct.
    E.   Record total number correct in score box.

SPELLING

1 Write child's name on spelling sheet.

2. Encourage child to try each word.

3. Use a sentence for the word only as needed. If a sentence is used, remember to repeat the spelling word after the sentence.

4 As child writes, copy spellings onto score sheet.

5 Scoring: After child leaves, assign points. (See appendix: "Developmental Spelling Scoring System.")

6 Transfer total points to score box.

PASSAGES READING

1. Tape-record all passages. Say child's name on tape before the first passage. Also, write each child's name on the appropriate side of the tape. Usually, three children can be recorded on one side of a 90 minute tape.

2. All students should begin at PP1 (The Storm). All students should attempt to read at least three passages.

3. Read introduction (in italics) to the student. Allow a moment for student to look at illustrations on first page.

4. <u>Begin timing</u> student as first word is read. End timing after last word is read.
5. Stop after a passage on which the student is clearly frustrated (below 80% accuracy).
6. <u>Errors</u> The following oral reading miscues should be marked and COUNTED AS ERRORS:

A. <u>Substitutions</u>   The boy went home.
B. <u>Insertions</u>   She went to school.
C. <u>Omissions</u>   She loves her mom.
D. <u>Teacher Help</u>   The elephant was big.
   (Wait <u>three</u> seconds before giving help.)

E. <u>Skipping a line</u> Have student go back to correct place immediately. Mark skip in margin and count as one error.

F. <u>Proper names</u>. If student misses the same proper name more than once, only one error is counted.

G. <u>Part of a word missed</u>. If a student mispronounces a full syllable of a word, it is counted as an error. Examples: If a student says "pi-pickle" (pronouncing the first syllable with a long *i*), it is scored as an error with a self-correction. If student says "pick-pickle", it is <u>not</u> an error, but only a repetition of part of the word. If a student makes a It sound before pronouncing "think" correctly, no error is recorded as a full syllable was not mispronounced.

H. <u>Reversing order of words</u>. If a student reads two words in reverse order (e.g., text reads: "He was too big;" student reads: "He was big, too"), mark as shown below and count as only <u>one</u> error.

7. <u>Self-corrections</u> The elephant was big. Self-corrected errors are not counted as errors.

He was too big.

8. <u>Repetitions</u> are NOT COUNTED AS ERRORS but are marked by underlining. Examples:
<u>She came</u> home late.   He was <u>being</u> silly.

9. <u>Accuracy Score</u>: Multiply the number of errors by the error quotient for the passage, then subtract this number from 100.

100 - (# of errors X error quotient)
Example from Preprimer passage:
4 errors X 1.4= 5.6, round off to 6
100 - 6 = 94% Accuracy

9. <u>Rate score</u>: Record time it takes student to read the passage. Convert minutes and seconds to total seconds. Use the formula provided on the score sheet for the passage to determine words per minute (wpm)

Example from 1-2 passage:
Reading time: 1 min. 34 sec; total seconds = 94
6000/94 = 63.8, round off to 64 words per minute (wpm)

10. <u>For each passage</u>, enter total errors, accuracy score, number of self corrections, and rate on the passage score sheet and on the cover score sheet for this student.

11. <u>When a tape is completed</u> and scores have been calculated, write examiner's name and school on the tape. Place tape and all score sheets for each student on that tape in a large manila envelope. Write the name of the school and the examiner's name on the envelope and close with clasp.

<u>CORRECT SPELLING</u> = 5pts.

SCORES FOR SAMPLE SPELLINGS

		<u>1 PT.</u>	<u>2 PTS.</u>	<u>3 PTS.</u>	<u>4 PTS.</u>
1.	BACK	b	bk, bc bake	bak, bac	backe
2.	FEET	v, f	ft, fit	fet	fete, feart
3.	STEP	s, c	sp, se, sa, st, setp, stp	sap, sep, stap, cap, ctep	stepe
4.	JUNK	g, j	gc, jk, jo gu, jike	guc, juc, joke, juke, gok, gonk, gnk	gunk, gunc junke
5.	PICKING	p	pc, pg, pn, pne	pecking, pekn, piking, peking	picking, pikig
6.	MAIL	m	ml, ma, mial	mal, mall, mel	male, maill, malle
7.	SIDE	s, c	sd, sed	sid, sod, sad sode, sade	sied, siad
8.	CHIN	c, i, g h, t	cn, ci, ce, cind, thei	cin, gin, hin, jin hen, thin, then, chen	chine
9.	DRESS	d, g, i r, s	ds, js, drs, gs	des, gas, das, dras dais, drres, gaas, gras gres, jas	dres, dresse
10.	PEEKED	p	pk, pikt, pe, pet, pen, peet, peke, pit, pct, pkt	pect, pekd, pekt, peekt	peked, peaced
11.	LAMP	l	lp, la, lm	lap, lam, lape, lmp	lampe
12.	ROAD	r, w	rd, ro, rodt, wd, romd	rod, wod	rode, rood, roid, roed
13.	PLANT	p	pt	pat, plat, plate	plante
14.	SHORT	s	st, chort, shrt, sot	shot, shote, sorte, sort	shorte
15.	GRABBED	g	gab, grad gbde, gd, gb	gabd, grabd	grabed

EXPLANATION OF SPELLING SCORES
FOR ALL WORDS

Left-right reversals (b-d) count as correct, up-down reversals (m-w) count as incorrect.

Beginning consonant (or appropriate substitution) = 1 pt.

Beginning and ending consonant (or appropriate substitutions) = 2 pts.

Beginning consonant and correct vowel (or appropriate substitutions) = 2 pts.

Beginning consonant, medial vowel and final consonant (or appropriate substitutions) = 3 pts.

Two vowels together in middle of word if first vowel is correct or the appropriate substitution ("dais" for dress) = 3 pts.

If long vowel is "marked" and all consonants are correct including blends and digraphs ("fete" or "feat" for feet) = 4 pts (first vowel must be correct).

Point deducted for extraneous consonants at the end of a word ("cind" for chin = 2 pts).

Point deducted for missing beginning consonant ("rs" for dress =1 pt.).

Point deducted for letters out of order ("tsap" for step = 2 pts.).

WORDS WITH SUFFIXES

For 3 pts., must have vowel (or appropriate substitution), beginning and ending consonants of the baseword, and the suffix must be represented by an appropriate letter ("pekn" for picking = 3 pts. but "peck" for picking = 2pts).
For 4 pts. must have correct vowel, correct consonants including blends and digraphs "marker," vowel and correct spelling for suffix (ed, ing).

EARLY STEPS WORD RECOGNITION TEST
Mid-year and End-of-Year
(For student to read from)

1.	cat	21.	leg
2.	is	22.	black
3.	like	23.	smile
4.	old	24.	dark
5.	your	25.	couldn't
6.	said	26.	because
7.	big	27.	shout
8.	not	28.	glass
9.	back	29.	paint
10.	sun	30.	children
11.	bird	31.	table
12.	saw	32.	stand
13.	feet	33.	gate
14.	lake	34.	pull
15.	hid	35.	spill
16.	about	36.	prize
17.	rain	37.	shoot
18.	how	38.	wrote
19.	window	39.	able
20.	mother	40.	change

School _____   Student _____

Examiner _____   # Sessions _____

Date _____   Month of 1st Session _____

Classroom Teacher _____   First Steps Teacher _____

WORD RECOGNITION SCORE ____   SPELLING SCORE _____

PASSAGE READING

	Emergent	Preprimer	Primer		1-2	2-1	2-2
Accuracy (%)	____	____	____		____	____	____
# Self-corrections	____	____	____		____	____	____
Rate	____	____	____		____	____	____

WORD RECOGNITION

1.	cat	_____	21.	leg	_____
2.	is	_____	22.	black	_____
3.	like	_____	23.	smile	_____
4.	old	_____	24.	dark	_____
5.	your	_____	25.	couldn't	_____
6.	said	_____	26.	because	_____
7.	big	_____	27.	shout	_____
8.	not	_____	28.	glass	_____
9.	back	_____	29.	paint	_____
10.	sun	_____	30.	children	_____
11.	bird	_____	31.	table	_____
12.	saw	_____	32.	stand	_____
13.	feet	_____	33.	gate	_____
14.	lake	_____	34.	pull	_____
15.	hid	_____	35.	spill	_____
16.	about	_____	36.	prize	_____
17.	rain	_____	37.	shoot	_____
18.	how	_____	38.	wrote	_____
19.	window	_____	39.	able	_____
20.	mother	_____	40.	change	_____

SPELLING

1.	back	_____
2.	feet	_____
3.	step	_____
4.	junk	_____
5.	picking	_____
6.	mail	_____
7.	side	_____
8.	chin	_____
9.	dress	_____
10.	peeked	_____
11.	lamp	_____
12.	road	_____
13.	plant	_____
14.	short	_____
15.	grabbed	_____

Name_____

1. _____

2. _____

3. _____

4. _____

5. _____

6. _____

7. _____

8. _____

9. _____

10. _____

11. _____

12. _____

13. _____

14. _____

15. _____

Student _____

Level: Emergent A
Title: The Storm

Introduction: Please read this book
called *The Storm*.

Here comes the cloud.

Here comes the wind.

Here comes the lightning.

Here comes the thunder.

Here comes the rain.

Here comes the rainbow.

and here comes...

the sun.

Words: 29
Errors: _____
Error Quotient: 3.4
Accuracy: ____%
Self Corrections: _____

Time: ___min.____sec.
Rate: 1740/____secs.=____wpm

Level: Preprimer A
Title: Look for Me

Introduction: Let's see what happens
in this book called *Look for Me*.

Mom looked for David
in the toy box.
"No, he's not here." she said.
She looked for him
up the chimney.
"No he's not here," she said.
She looked for him in the clock.
"No he's not here." she said.
She looked for him in the teapot.
"No he's not here." she said.
Where is that boy?
[Giggle, giggle.]
Mom looked for David under
the rug.
Here he is," she said.

* Do not count mistakes on
"giggle, giggle" as errors

Words: 69
Errors: _____
Error Quotient: 1.4
Accuracy: ____%
Self Corrections: _____

Time: ___min.____sec.
Rate: 1740/____secs.=____wpm

Level: Primer A

Title: "Clouds" <u>Mouse Tales</u>
(pp.18-23)

Introduction: *You may have seen clouds that look like animals or other things. Read this to see what pictures the little mouse and his mother see in the clouds.*

"Look!" said Mother. "We can see pictures

in the clouds." The little mouse and his

mother saw many pictures in the clouds.

They saw a castle...

a rabbit...

a mouse.

"I am going to pick flowers," said mother.

"I will stay here and watch the clouds,"

said the little mouse.

The little mouse

saw a big cloud in the sky.

It grew bigger and bigger

The cloud became a cat. The cat came

nearer and nearer to the little mouse.

"Help!" shouted the little mouse, and he

ran to his mother.

"There is a big cat in the sky!" cried /

Words:	100
Errors:	____
Error Quotient:	1.0
Accuracy:	___ %
Self Corrections:	____
Time:___ min. ____ sec.	
Rate: 6000/____ secs. =	____ wpm

Level: 1-2 A
Title: "Ice Cream" <u>Frog and</u>
   <u>Toad All Year</u> (pp.30-33)

Introduction: *Frog and Toad are*
very good friends. Lets see what
they are up to in this story called
"Ice Cream."

One hot summer day Frog and Toad sat by

the pond. "I wish we had some sweet, cold

ice cream," said Frog. "What a good idea,"

said Toad. "Wait right here, Frog. I will be

back soon." Toad went to the store. He

bought two big ice cream cones.

Toad licked one of the cones. "Frog likes

chocolate best," said Toad, "and so do I."

Toad walked along the path. A large, soft

drop of chocolate ice cream slipped down

his arm. This ice cream is melting in the

sun," said Toad.

Toad walked faster.   Many drops of

melting ice cream /

Words:	100
Errors:	____
Error Quotient:	1.0
Accuracy:	___ %
Self Corrections:	____
Time:___ min. ____ sec.	
Rate: 6000/____ secs. =	____ wpm

Level: 2-1 A
Title: <u>Daniel's Duck</u>
(pp.18-22)

Introduction: Daniel and his family lived long ago when people made many things by hand. Let's read about this family.

Every spring there was a fair in the valley. It was time for people to meet after the long winter. It was a time to show things that they had made. Sometimes they sold what they had made. Sometimes they traded with one another. Father knew how to make Indian moccasins.

On winter nights he made moccasins to take to the fair.

Mother cut pieces of cloth. She sewed them together to make a quilt.

"This will be a warm quilt for somebody's bed," she said. "I'll take it to the fair."

"I'm going to make a box for the /

Words:	100
Errors:	____
Error Quotient:	1.0
Accuracy:	___ %
Self Corrections:	____
Time:___ min. ____ sec.	
Rate: 6000/____ secs. =	____ wpm

Level: 2-2 A
Title: <u>Wild. Wild Wolves</u> **(pp.15-16)**

Introduction: *Let's read from this book that tells how real wolves live.*

A hungry wolf can eat 20 pounds of meat at a single meal. That's like eating one hundred hamburgers! To get all this meat, wolves usually hunt big animals like deer and moose. But a hungry wolf will chase and eat a rabbit or a mouse. It may even go fishing!

Wolves live in groups called packs. The pack members "talk" to each other with their bodies. When a wolf is scared, it holds its ears close to its head.

When a wolf is happy, it wags its whole tail. If it wags just the tip, watch out!

It is getting /

Words:	100
Errors:	____
Error Quotient:	1.0
Accuracy:	___ %
Self Corrections:	____
Time:___ min. ____ sec.	
Rate: 6000/____ secs. =	____ wpm

Early Steps
Learning From A Reader
Index